Did Lizzie Borden Axe For It?

A New Look At the Woman
and the Murder Case

D1478235

David Rehak

ISBN: 978-1-4357-1175-4
Angel Dust Publishing Group

New York

Did Lizzie Borden Axe For It?

Come from the four winds, O breath of God,
and breathe upon these slain,
so that they may live again.

Ezekiel 37:9

Dedicated to the memory
of the victims of this most disgusting and evil tragedy,
Andrew Jackson Borden (1822-1892) and Abby Durfee Gray
Borden (1828-1892).

Also in memory
of my cousin Honzik Vitasek (1971-1999),
whose tragic and horrendous death remains a mystery.
Vzpominame na tebe, Honziku.

Did Lizzie Borden Axe For It?

She is either the most injured of innocents or the blackest of monsters. She either hacked her father and stepmother to pieces with the furious brutality of the ogre in Poe's story of the Rue Morgue or some other person did it and she suffers the double torture of losing her parents and being wrongfully accused of their murders.

New York Sun, June 5, 1893

Regardless of whether Lizzie is guilty or innocent, if she hated her stepmother so much and was so mad at her dad, to ease the family tensions and live more happily I wonder why she and Emma didn't just move out of the Borden home to their own Ferry Street house? Perhaps then there would have been no murders.

Stanley Pipkin, Lizzie crime buff

Lizzie helped take off her father's shoes when the photo shows he had them on when murdered? Lizzie was looking for iron for a screen to fix which was found in no need of fixing? Lizzie said she heard a groan come from the house and then said she heard nothing? Lizzie took off her hat when she walked in to find Andrew yet Hyman Lubinsky said she had 'nothing on her head'? Lizzie testifying that the guest-room door was shut all morning so she couldn't have discovered her step-mother's dead body when she was up there but in fact the door was found open? Lizzie saying 'they' told her to change her dress after the murders when nobody did? The ominous 'prediction' to Alice Russell the night before the murders? The Winward [graveyard undertaker] funeral plans that

Did Lizzie Borden Axe For It?

Lizzie already had for her father and stepmother? The talk from Lizzie about claiming to know where Abby was and sending the maid Bridget up the front stairs to discover the body? We talk about reasons why Lizzie could have been guilty. But what reasons are there that may point to her being innocent? I couldn't think of any."

Sherry Chapman, Lizzie writer

Lizzie loved her father . . . she would have rather killed herself than kill her father.

Arnold Brown, Lizzie writer

Some folks said she didn't do anything to try and find the killer. She was like an unsightly spot. I think they wanted her to go away, but she showed her stubbornness and stayed, she didn't wanna live anyplace or anywheres but on the Hill with the smart set. Word on the street was that she said she was holding out that they'd find the killer and she wanted to be in Fall River to see the faces of all those who turned on her when the real killer was caught at last. And that was Lizzie's reason for stayin' and not movin' nowhere else, she said.

Edith C. Hart, lifelong resident of Fall River

Did Lizzie Borden Axe For It?

Lizzie Borden is just a famous person from history that people know. Make no mistake about it: she is a hook that will get people here [to Fall River]. If they ever solve that murder, we're sunk.

Robert Boiselle, president of the chamber of commerce

Miss Borden was not the sort of person one could believe guilty of such a crime as that with which she was charged. It is not the unemotional, grim, stocky and stalwart Lizzie Borden that I remember, but a quiet, reserved, frail little old-fashioned gentlewoman.

Nance O'Neil, actress and Lizzie friend

After the O.J. Simpson trial, I think a lot of people equate his acquittal to Lizzie's acquittal.

Jules Ryckebusch, founder of the Lizzie Borden Quarterly

Lizzie Borden was my friend. She was tried and she was acquitted. We don't talk about that anymore.

Mary Brigham, Lizzie friend

Did Lizzie Borden Axe For It?

If fingerprinting were used and DNA science were present then, she would have been convicted--it doesn't take a rocket scientist!

Diane Masek, Lizzie crime buff

Now what are we to say of the case? This: At a recent court convened according to the laws of the commonwealth of Massachusetts, the first party of the only two who could have committed the deed . . . [Lizzie Borden] was declared not guilty, and I have demonstrated . . . the absolute and entire innocence of the second party, leaving no grounds for any doubt. It, therefore, follows that no murder was committed.

Todd Lunday (pseudonym), Lizzie writer

An anonymous Borden relative speaks:
"By blood! If she did it, the old Borden nerve, grit, and cheek are not degenerated. No woman except a Borden could have done it, and yet it seems impossible that a woman could do it. I have watched her indomitable nerve and bearing with admiration, and I recalled Aunt Nannie Borden, who ran out when the bullets were flying, and kicked a wounded British redcoat and then tore up her skirts for wadding; and I remember that my poor old grandmother when a constable seized her broadcloth cloak for grandfather's rum bill, when he read his warrant and said: 'I seize this cloak,' she took him by the throat and said: 'God! And I seize you!' And he was glad to drop the cloak and git. So if this girl has done this thing it is the old Borden nerve and grit that carried her through, *and I predict*

Did Lizzie Borden Axe For It?

that she will not wilt. No, by blood."

Fall River Daily Globe, August 17, 1892

We were talking in the afternoon, me and Lizzie Borden, and I says, "I can tell you one thing you can't do," and she says, "Tell me what it is, Mrs. Reagan." I says, "Break an egg, Miss Borden," and she says, "Break an egg?" I says, "Yes." "Well," she says, "I can break an egg." I says, "Not the way I would tell you to break it." She says, "Well, what way is it, Mrs. Reagan?" So I told her that she couldn't break it the way I wanted her to break it, and I said I would bet her a dollar that she couldn't, and she said she would bet me a quarter, and in the afternoon someone fetched Lizzie an egg, and Miss Emma Borden was sitting down beside her, and I told Miss Emma Borden to get a little ways away, "Because," I said, "if she will break the egg the wrong way it will destroy your dress," and she did get the egg, and she got it in her hands, and she couldn't break it, and she says, "There," she says, "*that is the first thing that I undertook to do that I never could.*"

from the trial trestimony of Hannah Reagan, prison matron

You can't prove that Lizzie 'did it.'

**Maynard Bertolet, editor of the Lizzie Borden Quarterly
(in telephone conversation with the author)**

Did Lizzie Borden Axe For It?

CONTENTS

Did Lizzie Borden Axe For It?

The Lizzie Shrines

III.

Miscellaneous

IV.

Did Lizzie Borden Axe For It?

Did Lizzie Borden Axe For It?

Appendices

V.

Bibliography

Did Lizzie Borden Axe For It?

Introduction by the Author

To tease me, people like to pun on my last name when it comes to my writings on Lizzie Borden. Usually the joke has some witty wordplay to do with the words "hack" and "Rehak". I'm very fond of humor and joking myself, so I get a kick out of it too.

The Borden murders took place in Fall River. What is Fall River? It's an industrial city in southeastern Massachusetts, a port on Mount Hope Bay, at the mouth of the Taunton River. The city has numerous historical buildings and it's where many tourists come to see the famous battleship USS Massachusetts from World War 2. In 1656 the community was established by settlers hailing from Plymouth Colony. In 1811, the first cotton mill was established, and in time the city became well-known for its textile mills, which brought it prosperity well into the 1920's. The ancient Indian name for the area is Quequechan, which means "falling water."

Before we get into the details directly related to Lizzie, here is a curious incident worth recounting. Long before the Borden trial of 1893, an ancestor of Lizzie's named Thomas Cornell was tried and convicted of murdering his mother whom he allegedly hated. The "evidence" that sent him to his doom is beyond laughable, downright absurd. A man testified that he had had a dream in which Cornell's mother confessed to him that her son had killed her. This apparently was enough to convince the Salem-witch-style court and judges of the man's guilt. He was hanged.

I've been a careful and thoughtful scholar and enthusiast of the Borden case for quite a number of years now. This book is the product of about eight years of work (four years of study, two years of research, and two more years of writing and revision). I became hooked on Lizzie ever since 1996 when I saw the A&E television biography on her. Lizzie was the most average, unremarkable woman, and the most extraordinary, remarkable criminal or criminal suspect. Before she was accused of murder, she was a tiny grain of sand, an absolute nobody who no one took much notice of and who would have vanished from the world's memory like a candlelight. But after she was accused of murder, she became an unforgettable symbol and legend, an absolute somebody. What I find most interesting is the height of passionate feeling and passionate disagreement that she brings out in people, every kind of person. In fact, during the trial of Lizzie Borden, according to the *New York Times* it was estimated that about 1, 900 marriages ended in divorce because of the intense difference of opinion between husbands and wives that it created concerning Lizzie's innocence or guilt. The divide between those who believe she did the crime and those who don't sometimes runs very deep. There are also those who are still undecided, sitting on the fence, so to speak. These people are impressed by evidence that points either way, and find themselves unable to commit to a strong and sure stance. Did Lizzie Borden take an "axe"? Who's right and who's wrong? That, my friends, we do not know for 100% certain. In fact, so many years have passed with this mystery still unsolved, it's almost a certainty that we will *never* know for sure. But, as this book will reveal, there are certain probabilities in this case that should not be suppressed or ignored; there are certain probabilities that deserve scholarly consideration. Theories and ideas should be put on the table and each and every individual should be allowed to make his or her mind up about what they personally want to believe. As long as a theory isn't disproven, groundless or absurd in relation to the facts, it can be considered. We all need to be given the choice to agree or disagree.

There is still a rich harvest out there of new and rare fact and theory about the Lizzie case that awaits to be reaped. This book is an attempt to bring in some of that harvest.

Firstly, in the opening section, we will deal with just the bare facts of what we know happened that horrible day of August 4, 1892. Then, the theory that Lizzie committed the murders will be broadly examined, along with the theory that she was innocent of the crime. This will be followed by balanced and reasonable conclusions to be drawn from the arguments. Among other things, the second section will deal with my private correspondence with amateur Lizzie actress Sharon Sexton, who was present at the 1992 Centennial Conference on the Lizzie Borden case commemorating or celebrating (for lack of a better word!) the day of the murders in Fall River, and who made quite a stir with her unannounced and overwhelming visit to the Fall River Historical Society, where she confidently declared: "I'm Lizzie Borden!" One can only imagine the wry smile that ran across the museum curator, Michael Martin's, face. This section will deal with the truly unbelievable and as yet unsubstantiated story she told me about certain Lizzie items and documents she was allegedly allowed to handle from a "private collection," including, purportedly, the unpublished diary that she claims Lizzie kept for every year of her life; it is her belief that it has been kept "private" to protect Lizzie. The third section of this book will explore the infamous Second Street house and delve into the realm of the supernatural as I try to unearth what is behind the allegation that the house where Andrew and Abby Borden were murdered is haunted by strange noises, unexplainable occurrences, apparitions, and more. This section also covers the history of the Maplecroft and Swansea homes from the time that Lizzie lived there to now, and goes into detail about the Fall River Historical Society, which possesses the world's largest collection of items and materials related to Lizzie Borden. Her final resting place at Oak Grove Cemetery is also examined. Section four consists of works of non-fiction, fiction, humor and poetry, all to do with Lizzie and/or the Borden murder mystery. The fifth and final part of this book discusses Lizzie's will and includes her obituary, as well as a recommended reading section which may serve as a sort of road map for more Lizzie. It's a recommendation list of what I consider to be the most fun reading on the case, and what are largely believed by most experts to be the best Lizzie books/documents out there.

Now sit back and immerse yourself in the quiet, middle-class world of 92 Second Street, 1892, on the Thursday morning of August 4 that rocked the entire town, the whole country, and the very ends of the civilized world.

Did Lizzie Borden Axe For It?

The Morning of the Murders: A Comprehensive Chronology

August 4, 1892.

6:15 am   Bridget, the maid, is the first one up and dressed; she goes downstairs; she fetches firewood from the basement and heats up the stove.

6:20 am   John Morse comes downstairs from the guest-room where he has just spent the night.

6:30 am   Abby appears in the kitchen from the backstairs and tells Bridget to make breakfast.

6:40 am   Andrew comes downstairs; he takes his chamber-pot out the side screen door and dumps his "waste" outside under the barn.

7:00 am   Andrew, Abby and John Morse eat breakfast.

7:30   Bridget, having waited for them to finish eating, takes her breakfast.

7:30-8:45   Morse and Andrew relax in the sitting-room while Abby does the household dusting.

8:45 am   Andrew walks John Morse out the side screen door and asks him to come back later for "dinner" (lunch). John's response is not known.

8:50-55 am   Lizzie comes downstairs for breakfast. She then fetches some handkerchiefs and prepares them in the kitchen to iron.

8:55 am   Abby instructs Bridget to clean all the windows on the ground floor; Abby goes upstairs to change the pillow-cases in the guest-room.

9:00 am   Morse is seen at the post office dropping off a letter, and he then heads over to visit his niece and nephew, the Emerys, across town. Next-door neighbor Adelaide Churchill sees Andrew Borden leave the house.

9:00-9:30 am   Bridget cleans the breakfast dishes downstairs in the kitchen; Abby is murdered in the upstairs guest-room by repeated and penetrating strikes to the back of the skull by what is most likely a hatchet.

9:30 am   Bridget goes outside to start washing the windows. Lizzie calls to Bridget at the side screen door if she would like the door hooked; Bridget replies "no," and that she would be around.

9:00-10:20 am   Andrew goes to the barber shop to get shaved; sends a letter for Lizzie at the post office; makes brief walking trips to several banks.

9:30-10:30 am   Bridget cleans the windows from the outside.

9: 40 am   John Morse arrives at the Emery's house on 4 Weybossett Street.

10:20-10:30 am   Andrew stops off at a store Jonathan Clegg would be leasing from him.

10:30 am   Bridget goes inside and starts to do the other side of the windows.

10:40 am   Andrew tries to get into the Borden house through the side screen door, but it's locked; he is admitted in through the front door by Bridget.

10:45 am   Having spent a few minutes sitting in the dining-room, Andrew heads up into his bedroom for a sweater and then comes back down to sit on the sofa in the sitting-room.

10:50 am   Lizzie informs Bridget of a sale at *Sargeant's*, a store downtown. Bridget replies that she might go and check it out. Lizzie says that she might be leaving the house too.

10:55 am   Bridget has finished the windows and she retires to her attic room for a short nap.

10:55-11:00 am   A buggy is spotted parked on the corner between the Borden and Kelly yards.

14

Did Lizzie Borden Axe For It?

10:55-11:05 am   Andrew is murdered on the sitting-room sofa by repeated and penetrating strikes to the face and side of the head by a similar/same instrument as was used on his wife, Abby.

11:10 am   Lizzie summons Bridget with the frantic news that someone has "killed father." Bridget rushes downstairs and out of the house to get Doctor Bowen, but he isn't home, so she goes to Alice Russell, a long-time friend of Emma and Lizzie, who lives nearby.

11:15 am   Mrs. Churchill spots a distressed-looking Lizzie standing by the side screen door and calls out to her with concern. The Fall River Police receives a phone call about a fight or stabbing at the Borden house.

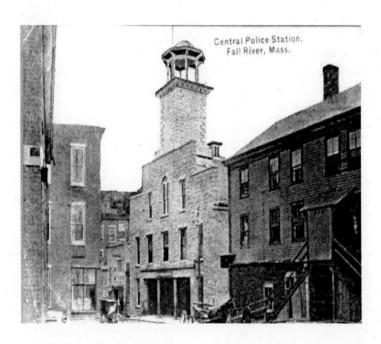

The Fall River Central Police Station. On the morning of the murders, most of the police force happened to be off-duty out on an annual excursion--private collection

Did Lizzie Borden Axe For It?

11:20 am   John Morse leaves the Emery house. Police officer Allen is sent by Marshal
Hilliard to examine the "stabbing" at the Borden house; he sprints and arrives and finds Andrew's dead body; he rushes back to the police station and nervously stammers to the city marshal what he has just witnessed.

11:25 am   Doctor Bowen arrives by carriage and examines the corpse; he is appalled by the degree of mutilation. He leaves immediately to telegram Lizzie's older sister Emma that "father is very ill." Emma is staying with friends in Fairhaven, a nearby town.

11:30 am   Abby Borden's dead body is found.

11:35-40 am   Officers Doherty, Wixon, and Mullaly arrive at the house. Numerous other officers will follow.

11:40-50 am   John Morse arrives at the house but doesn't go inside right away; he loiters in the backyard eating a pear. When he finally goes inside and learns of the murders, he gasps: "what kind of God do we have that would allow this!"

Works consulted:
Faye Musselman, *Historic Timeline-Chronology of Lizzie Borden*
Leonard Rebello, *Lizzie Borden, Past & Present*
Preliminary Hearing of the Lizzie Borden Murder Case
Superior Court Trial Transcript of the Lizzie Borden Murder Case
Neilson Caplain, Lizzie Borden Murder Case Chronology, *Lizzie Borden Quarterly*, January/July 2001

Did Lizzie Borden Axe For It?

John Morse--courtesy Faye Musselman

Did Lizzie Borden Axe For It?

Purported to be a photo of Andrew Borden--from the Swansea Historical Society Collection, courtesy Faye Musselman

Did Lizzie Borden Axe For It?

I. The Murders

The Bare Facts

Here at the outset we are only concerned with the facts--what all sides agree on. Just the essential facts.

According to the trial testimony of the Borden maid Bridget "Maggie" Sullivan, at ten or eleven minutes past 11 o'clock, she heard Lizzie from the rear staircase holler up to her in a very loud voice: "Maggie, come down quick! Father's dead! Someone came in and killed him!" Bridget came rushing down from her attic bedroom to find a distraught Lizzie, who ordered her to go to Doctor Seabury Bowen's house across the street. But Bridget came back with the news that Doctor Bowen wasn't home, so Lizzie sent her to go get their close friend, Alice Russell, who lived down the street.

In the meantime, Lizzie's next-door neighbor Mrs. Adelaide Churchill was just returning from grocery shopping and saw Lizzie standing at the side screen door. Lizzie appeared frazzled and Mrs. Churchill, looking out of one of her kitchen windows, called out to her what was wrong. Lizzie replied: "Oh Mrs. Churchill, please do come over!" and that someone had murdered her father. Mrs. Churchill asked Lizzie where she had been and she replied that she was in the barn. To those who asked, Lizzie said she had been looking for lead to make "sinkers" for fishing or iron to fix the screen door.

19

Did Lizzie Borden Axe For It?

Andrew Borden

Did Lizzie Borden Axe For It?

Crime photo of Andrew Borden

Did Lizzie Borden Axe For It?

Autopsy photo of Andrew Borden's face--courtesy Eric Stedman

Did Lizzie Borden Axe For It?

Abby Borden

Did Lizzie Borden Axe For It?

Crime photo of Abby Borden--from Edwin H. Porter, The Fall River Tragedy

Did Lizzie Borden Axe For It?

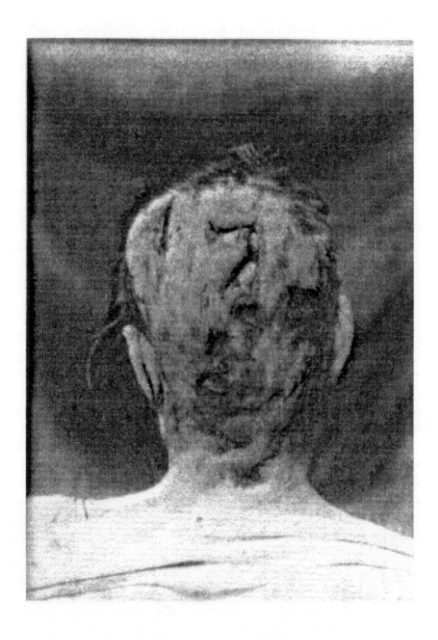

Autopsy photo of back of Abby Borden's head

Did Lizzie Borden Axe For It?

Dr. Bowen arrived and found Andrew's bloody, mutilated corpse on the sitting-room sofa. He later identified eleven distinct cuts to the face and left side of the head which could only have been delivered by a sharp blade. The first people on the scene, aside from the doctor, were his wife Phoebe Bowen, Alice Russell, who came right over after a quick change of clothes, and of course Mrs. Churchill and Bridget Sullivan.

The police was quickly notified by John Cunningham, a newspaper seller who just happened to be closeby, that there had been some kind of domestic disturbance or "a stabbing" committed at the Borden house. Although most of the police force was out on an excursion, Officer Allen, a first patrolman was sent by the city marshal to the house at 11:15 AM to investigate the validity of the report. Allen ran into the house, witnessed the body of Andrew Borden, and ran back to the station in fright, stammering to Marshal Rufus Hilliard that a gruesome murder had taken place.

Meanwhile, Lizzie sat in the kitchen being consoled by the other ladies, who fanned her. She no longer seemed very distraught, just without emotion. She had always been characterized as an unemotional person and her friends and acquaintances made nothing of it. But her calm and placid (and what seemed to them undisturbed) demeanor appeared strange to the police officers and others who were in the house that day.

Suddenly, in the midst of all this, Bridget asked about Mrs. Borden (Abby). Lizzie replied that Abby had received a note to go out but believed she had heard her come in, and would she (Bridget) go upstairs and check? Bridget was afraid and refused to go alone, so Mrs. Churchill volunteered to go with her. They slowly went up the front stairs, Bridget first. Once her eye was level with the adjoining guest-room floor, Bridget looked over and through the open or half-open door saw the large, lifeless body of Mrs. Borden on the floor. Mrs. Churchill came running down. "Is there another?" asked Alice Russell. Bridget came down after a quick close-up look at the victim, and it was confirmed that there were now two dead bodies, not one.

Upon closer examination, 19 cuts were found on the body of Abby Borden, all but one to the back of the head. Abby was found on the floor with her hands underneath her and her face in a pool of dark and congealed blood. The brussels carpet was so soaked through in fact that the blood-stain puddle could not later be washed out.

The blood on Abby's wounds was thick, dark and dry, while her husband's wounds were still dripping red from his face. Both murders were a horrendous sight to the eye. It was later determined by various Harvard professors, all doctors, that Abby had died at around 9:30 AM, while Andrew it was estimated had died shortly before his body was discovered, around 11 o'clock AM.

Work cited and/or consulted:
The Superior Court Trial Transcript, Vol. 1 & 2, pp. 1-1930

Did Lizzie Borden Axe For It?

The side entry next to the side screen door where Lizzie yelled upstairs to the maid Bridget that someone had "killed father"-- courtesy Faye Musselman

Did Lizzie Borden Axe For It?

Lizzie Didn't Do It?

Believers in Lizzie's guilt always point to a dress-buring incident on Sunday three days after the murders when Lizzie tore up and burned in the kitchen stove a dress which had been accidentally stained with paint several months back when the house was being re-painted and Lizzie was supervising the workmens' job. Emma and others said that Lizzie routinely burned old and unwearable clothes in the kitchen stove, and indeed this was common practice in the 19th c. The dress that she burned in the kitchen three days after the murders was known to be soiled with paint which wouldn't come off, so she casually ripped it apart and burned it up. She did this in broad daylight while the police were around the premises and while Emma and Alice Russell were around to observe her; she didn't do it at night in secret as one would expect a guilty person to do. Several months before the murders, the dressmaker Mary Raymond, while she was staying at the Borden house for a week working on some dresses for the Borden women, remembered once seeing Lizzie rip up a dress in her presence and mention that she intended to burn it. So clearly this was an innocent habit of Lizzie's.

The argument that Lizzie didn't "do it" is centered on the fact that, first of all, no one witnessed the crimes, therefore we can't be 100% sure who did them. Second of all, Lizzie claims she was downstairs the whole time within the span that it is believed her step-mother was killed upstairs; she also claims she was in the barn loft when her father must have been slain. None of these claims

29

were discredited during the trial. Furthermore, there was no blood found on her hair or clothes except for a very miniscule spot on the back of her petticoat, not the front. This was explained away as coming from her "period" which she had been suffering from until the day before the murders. And what is perhaps even more suggestive of Lizzie's innocence--there was no murder weapon found at either crime scene. Also, Doctor Dolan testified at trial that the victims' wounds came from a left-handed killer, and Lizzie was right-handed. There were potential weapons, especially an old hatchet with a broken handle found in the cellar and a weather-worn hatchet found on the roof of a neighbor's shed in the backyard which was recognized by a workman as one he had lost, but neither of these hatchets were at the scene of the crimes and none of them were ever proven to be the murder weapon. There was gold "gilt" found in Abby's wounds suggesting that a new hatchet was used, which the handleless hatchet was not. In fact, lead prosecutor Hosea Knowlton himself wasn't entirely convinced that the handleless hatchet was the murder weapon, though he presented it at trial to help his case. So if there was no murder weapon in the vacinity, how could it possibly be that Lizzie Borden committed the murders?

According to Lizzie, she came downstairs that morning a little before 9 and went into the cellar and then into the kitchen. Her father and the guest of the previous night, Uncle Vinnicum Morse, had left the house. She ate a few cookies and drank some coffee while reading the *Providence Journal*. During her breakfast, or snack as it might more correctly be termed, Lizzie went up and got her ironing board and brought it into the dining-room. She had a few handkerchiefs she wanted to even out. Lizzie says she saw and heard no one in any part of the house at this time. From time to time, she took a break from ironing and ate her snack when she was waiting for the irons to get hot.

At 9:30 she went over to the screen door at the side of the house and asked Bridget if she wanted the door hooked. Bridget replied that she would be around and that the door may be left unhooked. For most of the time from 9:30 to about 10:30, the murderer could have gotten into the house through the side screen door when he saw that Bridget wasn't looking or wasn't around to see him. Then, after killing his second and last victim, he could have slipped out just as sneakily without necessarily being spotted.

Hyman Lubinsky, an ice cream peddler slowly driving his buggy past the Borden house, spotted a woman who was not Bridget coming from the direction of the barn towards the porch stairs of the side screen door about five or six minutes after 11 o'clock. Lizzie says she went into the barn almost as soon as her father got home, spending some 20-30 minutes there. If Lubinsky saw her when he says he did and if Lizzie was the woman he saw, then her story is quite consistent as far as the time goes--10:50 AM to 11:10 AM = 20 minutes. Lizzie was adamant that it was more like 20 minutes than 30. Her story fits.

So if not Lizzie, who committed the murders? It's a long list of suspects, from the plausible to the downright absurd. There were and have been literally dozens of these suspects. Some of them can be discounted with great or relative ease. For example, there is the prominent theory from Arnold Brown's *Lizzie Borden: The Legend, The Truth, The Final Chapter* that an illegitimate son of Andrew Borden allegedly named William S. Borden wanted to be acknowledged in Andrew's will, and when Andrew refused, Billy didn't axe him twice (sorry, I couldn't resist!). A woman named Ellen Eagan, who felt sick on the morning of the murders and vomited in the Kelly yard beside the Borden property, allegedly saw a man exit the side screen door of the Borden house on the morning of the murders. It is also alleged that she was told to keep quiet about it after Mayor Coughlin, Marshal Hilliard and Police Captain Harrington had decided that Lizzie was their suspect. Though it makes a great story, this theory has been discredited (see *The Latest on the William "Billy" Borden Story*). But a few of the suspect theories present tantalizing possibilities. Another theory is that Doctor Bowen himself may have committed or had a hand in the murders, the idea being that there was animosity between him and Andrew and that Andrew had treated him rudely the day before when Abby went to see the doctor and Andrew yelled: "My money shan't pay for it [the doctor's visit]!"--that perhaps being the last straw. Another common enough theory, first proposed by Edward Radin in *Lizzie Borden: The Untold Story*, is that Bridget had the opportunities to kill both Abby and Andrew Borden, though the facts suggest she would have needed quite a degree of luck not to be spotted by Lizzie. It has also been proposed by Frank Spiering in his *Lizzie* that Emma did it, though there are questions about whether she could have returned to Fairhaven in time to receive Dr. Bowen's telegram telling her that her parents were "ill." Still, there are many other suspects, a few whose names are not even known, and although some have been all but discredited, there are others who continue to linger and fascinate.

The entire list, more or less, consists of these names: John V. Morse, William S. Borden, Joseph W. Carpenter, Jonathan Clegg, Daniel Sullivan, Emma Borden, Hiram C. Harrington, Seabury Bowen, David M. Anthony, Jr., "Me and Brownie" Everett Brown and Thomas Barlow, Charles Davis, Alfred Johnson, Edward Barrett, Israel Hyman, Antonio Auriel, Peter Cooper, William L. Bassett, Jose Carreiro, Peleg Brightman, Alfred Smith, and Charlie Peckham. Based on the scientific opinion at the time, it was surmised by the medical experts that the blows that struck the victims were such as could have been inflicted by someone of "average" strength, even a woman. It has therefore even once been suggested that the killer was a woman other than Lizzie or Bridget! About 10 months before the murders, Mrs. Durfee of Second Street heard a man shout at Andrew Borden: "You have cheated me and I'll fix you for it!" (*Lizzie Borden, Past & Present*, p. 522). A man came to the Borden house on the morning of the murders (*Witness*

Did Lizzie Borden Axe For It?

Statements, p. 2). Sarah Harte and Delia Manley noticed a strange man standing by the gate of the Borden property between 9:50 and 10 o'clock. Doctor Benjamin Handy spotted a nervous well-dressed individual walking down Second Street as well, who was later supposedly identified according to the *Fall River Daily Herald* of August 11. About 10:30 Dr. Handy saw a pale, agitated young man between Dr. Kelly's and Mr. Wade's grocery store going south. At the preliminary hearing and trial, Handy said he was ghastly white, a stranger with wild eyes. He sported a small black moustache and looked desperate. About 10:30 Officer Hyde saw a 30-year-old man, 5' 5" tall, with a slight build, about 130 lbs, light gray suit, hat, and unusually white face like a man who spent most of his time in a cellar. The man looked intensely nervous, with an odd facial appearance indicative of an intense effort to repress excitement. In fact, to a *Boston Herald* reporter on the 10th, Hyde said he noticed this peculiar-looking man loitering about in front of the Borden premises. About 10:55-11:00, Mark P. Chase saw an open box buggy with a high top seat standing right by the tree at the corner of the Kelly-Borden properties. Chase had been there all forenoon and had not seen the buggy before this. A man with a brown hat and black coat was in the buggy. Chase didn't see him leave. Between 10 and 11, a 12-year-old boy named Pete Kerouack, according to the *Boston Herald* of the 5th, noticed a man jumping the back fence between the Borden and Chagnon yards. The man was tall and well-built, wore a light soft hat, and some kind of russet shoes. A few seconds later, Kerouack claimed to hear a noise like someone screaming for help from the Borden house. Kerouack wasn't called by either team at the trial. Then almost two weeks after the murders on August 16, a farmer named Joseph Lemay saw a blood-smeared individual holding a hatchet, muttering, "poor Mr. Borden." When the man saw Mr. Lemay, he held the hatchet up threateningly and Lemay stood his ground. This lasted for some time, and then the man turned around and ran off. Simply put, any number of

Did Lizzie Borden Axe For It?

suspicious types could plausibly have committed the murders and gotten away with it given the right ideal circumstances and the right amount of luck. Also, some Lizzie scholars like George Quigley have theorized quite interestingly that Lizzie, Emma, and Uncle Morse hired a killer for fear that they were being written out of Andrew's will.

If Lizzie killed her father, she only had about 10-15 minutes to wash the bloodstains off her body and change clothes before calling down Bridget. Nearly impossible, almost unimaginable. Changing into a Victorian dress in itself was a slow and tedious process, sometimes requiring assistance.

Lizzie was a member of church charity, a Sunday school teacher, a reputedly kind Christian woman who allowed small children to pick pears from her father's yard. According to Mrs. Handy, she was a woman who was generous and benevolent with both friend and stranger alike (involved in charity volunteerism, etc), who had a definite soft spot for people's suffering and need. Why would she commit the most heinous double murder in Fall River history? What for? Her father and stepmother were old and close to death as it was--what would have been the use of killing them? Andrew had no will that we know of which would leave everything or even a large share of his estate to Abby. We simply know nothing of any such will. Rumors don't prove a thing.

How could Lizzie have committed the murders when by most accounts she loved her father? She had given him her high school ring when she was 16, as a symbol of their special bond, which he "wore . . . on his pinky."

34

Did Lizzie Borden Axe For It?

The facts in her favor:

1) Lizzie was known to be in the habit of burning clothes that was old or for other reasons no longer wearable, and therefore there is nothing suspicious about the burning of the paint-smeared dress.

2) Arguably no blood on Lizzie.

3) No human blood on any of the hatchets/axes found in the house.

4) No proven murder weapon found.

5) A doctor testified the killer was left-handed; Lizzie was right-handed.

6) Lizzie was probably seen by the ice cream merchant Hyman Lubinsky coming towards the side of the house from the barn a few minutes after 11 o'clock, which corresponds with and is consistent with Lizzie's account that she had been in the barn and then came back inside at that point in time to find her father murdered.

7) Consistent trial testimony and newspaper reports from several eye-witnesses about a white-faced man dressed in a dark or grey coat seen on or around the Borden property; other suspicious men seen as well.

8) Lizzie likely didn't have enough time to commit the last murder, clean and hide the hatchet, and then wash up and change.

9) Lizzie's friends/advocates argued that she was a good, blameless, church-going woman who came from a good respectable family, and girls like that just don't kill people, especially with such exceptional brutality.

Works cited and/or consulted:
The Superior Court Trial Transcript for the Lizzie Borden Murder Case, Vol. 1 & 2
The Preliminary Hearing for the Lizzie Borden Murder Case

Did Lizzie Borden Axe For It?

The Inquest Upon the Deaths of Andrew J. and Abby D. Borden, August 9 - 11, 1892, Volume I & II

David Kent. *Forty Whacks: New Evidence in the Life and Legend of Lizzie Borden*

Leonard Rebello, *Lizzie Borden, Past & Present*

Richard Powers, *Death of a Massachusetts Trojan*, Chief of Police, Vol. IV, no. 4, July/August, 1989

Arnold R. Brown, *Lizzie Borden: The Legend, The Truth, The Final Chapter*

Edward D. Radin, *Lizzie Borden: The Untold Story*

Frank Spiering, *Lizzie*

The Witness Statements for the Lizzie Borden Murder Case

Fall River Daily Herald, August 11, 1892

The Boston Herald, August 5 and 10, 1892

The Washington Post, July 13, 1998

Naedine Joy Hazell, *Disputed Verdict on Lizzie Borden*

Fall River Evening News, August 10, 1892

Did Lizzie Borden Axe For It?

Lizzie Did It?

Immediately after discovering her father's dead body and calling Bridget down, Lizzie did something you wouldn't expect--or rather, she *didn't do* something you would expect any woman to do. Instead of running out of the house in terror that the killer may still be inside waiting to strike yet again, she stayed in the house behind the screen door. She didn't even join Bridget and run with her for help as any other woman would very likely do in the same situation. Either she was remarkably brave, or . . . !

For those who believe Lizzie guilty, the seeds of their doubt about her innocence were scattered around by none other than Lizzie herself through her confusing and self-incriminating inquest testimony. Lizzie just seemed unable to keep her story straight, changing her answers, being evasive, inaccurate, and so on. At one point she said she was upstairs in her bedroom when her father came home, then she said she was on the stairs in the front hall when he arrived; then she supposedly remembered that, no, in fact she must have been in the kitchen instead when her father was let in through the locked front door by the maid Bridget. But Bridget said she heard Lizzie laugh aloud from what sounded to her to be the staircase landing. Lizzie Borden playwright and researcher Eric Stedman in his fine annotation of the inquest testimony on his site **darksites.com/souls/horror/lizzieborden** gives a good account of "Lizzie's contradictions, improvisations and falsehoods in her inquest testimony." When Knowlton tried to ask Lizzie how it was

37

that she didn't see Abby downstairs at any time (even to go out to see a sick friend, since Lizzie alleges that Abby had received a note to go see someone), Lizzie responds that Abby could have gone downstairs and outside through the side screen door undetected by her when she, Lizzie, was briefly in the cellar. But how likely is it that Abby would leave the house exactly when Lizzie went downcellar for a few short minutes? Not likely. And Lizzie neither heard nor saw Abby leave the house. Furthermore, Mr. Stedman correctly points out: "For Lizzie to have been not guilty of the murders, the killer must have entered the house and done away with Mrs. Borden soundlessly during this time as well. But how could Lizzie's phantom 'enemy' have known exactly when Lizzie would visit the cellar?" As for this note that Abby supposedly got from a sick friend, Lizzie and Lizzie alone was the originator of that story; this fact was brought out by the Prosecution in the trial. Bridget, Alice Russell, and Doctor Bowen all heard of this "mystery note," but it came from Lizzie and Lizzie said that she burned the note in the stove. No one saw a note, no one saw her burn it, but for some unknown reason she says she burned it. Oh how convenient. It is highly probable that this note never existed and was used simply as an explanation to give Lizzie a good excuse for not discovering the dead and battered body of her mother in the house--in other words, Lizzie wants us to believe that Abby was out to visit this "sick friend" and not lying dead in the guest-room for nearly two hours with Lizzie in the house the whole time, and no other known person except Lizzie having gone up the front stairs before the bodies were discovered. Of course, we know from forensics that most likely Abby had been lying dead for one to two hours in that room, so Lizzie's story about Abby going out was clearly a fabricated lie. Another time, Lizzie said that she never saw Bridget after she let her father in, but Bridget's testimony bears out that it was then that Lizzie approached her by telling her there was a sale of "cheap goods" [dress material] at a downtown department store named

Did Lizzie Borden Axe For It?

Seargent's. And the list goes on. Altogether, Knowlton caught Lizzie in some 30 or so inaccuracies, contradictions, and downright lies. Most interestingly, Lizzie said that she had helped take her father's shoes off when he went to relax on the sofa in the sitting-room, yet the crime photo of his corpse shows that Andrew's shoes were still on when he was murdered! Lizzie apologists have tried to explain away Lizzie's conflicting statements by saying that on the three days of her inquest testimony, she had been given various doses of morphine at bedtime to calm her down and help her sleep, and that therefore she was in a drugged state of mind at the inquest and not able to think properly. But the medical fact is that the dose would have worn off by the time she took the stand the next day because each time it was taken intravenously, not orally (*A Private Disgrace*, p. 204).

Lizzie had murder on her mind; she had premeditated murder by going to pharmacist Eli Bence's drugstore on the corner of South Main and Columbia Streets to purchase a strong deadly poison called prussic acid, claiming she needed it to clean moths off of a sealskin cape, for which purpose it can hardly be used, since it is likely that the acid would sooner ruin the material than clean it, and there are infinitely better methods to clean a sealskin cape than the use of such a dangerous substance. Indeed, on page 129 of *A Private Disgrace*, we are informed that s*ealskin is and was well-known to have "natural immunity to moths (insect eggs do not hatch in it)*," therefore it is completely implausible that Lizzie wanted to buy it for the reason that she gave--to clean off moths. The pharmacist denied her illogical request. He and two of his assistants later positively identified Lizzie as the woman who had requested the item at their store, yet Lizzie denied that she had tried to make the purchase; she even claimed not to know where the drugstore was even though it was located just a few minutes' walk from her house and had been there for 14 years! There was a similar incident four years before the murders, when Lizzie had attempted to buy chloroform, another deadly poison, to kill a cat. This was confirmed by Walter J. Brow of Brow's Drug Store (*Lizzie Borden: Past & Present*, p. 81). So, Lizzie killed or attempted to kill with poison even before the prussic acid story hit the fan, although her victim was not human. This begs the question: then did she ever use a hatchet on any living thing before the murders? According to Abby's niece, Mrs. Abby Whitehead Potter, her mother had told her that Lizzie once killed a cat by chopping off its head with a hatchet. Then, on page 23 of *Goodbye Lizzie Borden* by Robert Sullivan, we have the following from Mrs. Potter's own mouth: "So the cat went in where Lizzie was entertaining and she took it out and shut the door again, and it came back . . . Lizzie Borden finally excused herself and went downstairs--took the cat downstairs--and put the carcass on the chopping block and chopped its head off. My aunt [Abby Borden] . . . for days wondered where the cat was--all she talked about. Finally Lizzie said, 'You go downstairs and you'll find your cat.' My aunt did." There is a high level of irony here. If Lizzie can buy and use poison or a hatchet on an animal (cat), can we not see her attempting to do the same to a human being(s) she is angry with or bitterly hates?

For the last 10 years or so leading up to the murders, relations between Abby and "the girls" Lizzie and Emma were getting worse and worse, especially between Abby and Emma, though Lizzie made it clear to one of her tourist companions Anna Borden on her return boat ride from her European Tour in November 1890 that she herself was not looking forward to returning to her household (*Lizzie*, p. 145). Furthermore, in May of 1892, just months before the murders, Lizzie told her dressmaker Mary Reynolds that "She [Abby] is a mean old thing and we hate her; we have little to do with her. I stay in my room most of the time." Then in late July, 1892 only about a week or two before the murders, Lizzie was apparently heard by Carrie M. Poole to say that, presumably because of Abby, she didn't know if she or Emma would get anything in the event of their father's death (*Inquest*, p. 144). This was a very interesting thing for Lizzie to have said such a short time before the murders, before she inexplicably cut short a vacation she was on and returned home, while Emma went on to visit some friends out of town, the Brownells. Miss Carrie was sister to Lizzie's old school friend, Augusta Tripp, and at the Inquest Mrs. Tripp, loyal to Lizzie, tried to downplay what Carrie heard Lizzie say by saying "she [my sister] is very feeble indeed" etc. In other words, Tripp was suggesting: "dont take anything my sister said seriously, she's just feeble-minded." But that's not a good enough explanation. We know about the problems in the Borden household; it seems likely that Lizzie *did* say that she didn't know if she would get anything if her father died. Carrie may have been "feeble", but she wasn't deaf, she did have ears to hear with and no reason to lie, and it seems likely that she did hear Lizzie say it. This just adds to Lizzie's motive to kill for the inheritance lest Abby should get it.

The tension reached a boiling point just 5 years before the murders. Unbeknownst to Lizzie and Emma, Andrew did in fact financially help Abby buy out the other half of the title of the property at 45 Fourth Street of which she had already owned the first half. This infuriated "the girls", especially because Andrew seemed to go to some length to conceal this generosity towards Abby from them; they saw the act as very uncharacteristic of their stingy father and a clear indication that Abby was having her way with him and was trying to get his fortune for herself and her relatives. To appease them, he gave them their deceased grandfather's house on Ferry Street, which they rented out.

Although there was never any physical proof of a will and some have theorized that the Borden family attorney, who was also Lizzie's defense lawyer named Andrew Jennings, may have destroyed any such will, John Morse testified at trial that there was, indeed, a will--that Andrew Borden had a will. John Morse was close with Andrew and knew his financial dealings, as they both purportedly liked to talk intimately about each other's business affairs. If there was a will leaving much of the inheritance to Abby and her family, then Lizzie would have had a strong motive to kill Abby--and then even Andrew--if she suspected that he would suspect her. That seems likely, since the previous summer Abby's dressing-room had been broken into and certain valuables, including jewellery, a watch, and *horse-car tickets* had been stolen while Lizzie was in the house. Again, the culprit was never identified. *But* certain men who were found by police to be selling these tickets and not entitled to them told the officers that Lizzie Borden had given the tickets to them. Andrew found out about this, and to protect Lizzie he used the excuse that "I am afraid the police will not be able to find the real thief", and asked Chief Hilliard to discontinue the investigation. Knowing that Lizzie had stolen from her step-mother only the year before, Andrew would probably have suspected that Lizzie was behind Abby's murder if he had lived to find out about it!

. At the time leading up to the murders, there was a rumor (or something more than a rumor) going around town that Andrew was preparing to sign over the property of Swansea to either Abby or John Morse, or both. Uncle Morse had stayed at the Borden house 5 years previously at the time that Andrew gave "the girls" the Ferry Street house. Now he was back again, this time presumably to advise or negotiate with Andrew over the transfer of the Swansea farms, which he would use for his horses, as he was a horsetrader by profession. On Wednesday afternoon, on the day before the murders, Lizzie heard her father and Morse discussing something downstairs at length. Author Victoria Lincoln believes that Lizzie overheard their conversation about the transfer of the Swansea deed to Morse or Abby and became upset and "worked up" over it. Then, just hours later, a highly agitated Lizzie went to Alice Russell claiming that her father had an enemy and that she feared the house would be burned down over their heads; she believed that their milk and bread were being poisoned and she predicted that something really horrible would happen in her household. Right the next morning, it did!

One of the controversies in the Borden case revolves around the question about which dress Lizzie was wearing on the day of the murders. We know she changed into a cheap "pink wrapper" dress at about noon, claiming that she had been asked to, although there is no proof of this and no one stepped forward to say that they had asked her to change, according to Alice Russell's trial testimony. Did Lizzie have on the Bengaline silk that her defense team argued she had on that fateful morning, *or* was she wearing a cotton Bedford cord? Other than the fact that the Bengaline was a fancy dress which was usually only worn when one was going out, not staying home and doing housework like ironing, there is real collaborating testimonial proof--and quite a bit of it--that Lizzie had in fact worn the Bedford cord instead, and that one or two witnesses, like Lubinsky and Bowen, had in fact mistaken the dark-blue Bengaline for the light-blue Bedford cord because, although white and light-blue, the Bedford dress had a "dark figure"; it has been suggested that the skirt and belt part of the cord were dark or dark-blue while the rest was a much lighter blue, according to Emma's trial testimony. It also had a "dark navy blue print on it" Mrs. Churchill testified. As I say, except for Doctor Bowen and his wife, every other witness who was with Lizzie at close quarters right after the murders testified to Lizzie having worn a dress whose description is in line with the Bedford cord; their testimony is consistent-- "light blue or white ground work . . . a cotton dress . . . (Mrs. Churchill); "It was a blue dress with a sprig on it . . . light blue" and that the sprig at the front of the dress was a darker blue (Bridget Sullivan); "I thought she had a light blue dress . . ." (Officer Doherty). Others testified to the same thing. In any future book on the case, it is this author's hope that drawings or photos of these two different dresses will be included, as the

Did Lizzie Borden Axe For It?

Victorian descriptions of them are not always clear to our modern 21st Century understanding. The point is, the Bengaline, which was presented at trial as the dress she claimed to have worn that morning, was not "light blue" by any possible definition, it was *not* the dress she had worn on the morning of the murders. Again, Lizzie had sought to deceive. And thanks to the defense testimony of the Bowens, she managed to produce enough doubt and confusion in the jury about the dresses.

Purported to be a photo of Alice Russell in old age (circa-1920's). She testified to seeing Lizzie burn a dress smeared with paint and perhaps blood just 3 days after the murders-- private collection

Did Lizzie Borden Axe For It?

The police conducted search after search in the days that followed the crime but the Bedford cord wasn't found. Where it disappeared to from Thursday afternoon to Sunday morning we will never truly know. Emma said it was hanging in the closet at the top of the front staircase on Saturday. Could the police have been so meticulous about checking Lizzie's bedroom and the other rooms that they overlooked or poorly examined what was hanging in this hallway closet? It's a possibility. Another consideration worth bearing in mind is that by the time the officers got to that closet, any blood-stains on it would have been brown. Dry blood on the fabric of the dress would have looked like dirt. There is no difference in appearance. The dress, if it was stained with blood at all (no one saw any stains on Lizzie's dress) would have been only lightly dabbed or sprinkled with blood. It appears that when she killed her victims, especially in the case of Andrew but also Abby, she wasn't splattered with blood at all. Take for instance the murder of her father--almost all the blood appeared on the wall and ceiling. Virtually none of it was on the carpet floor. Lizzie got little or no blood on her. At the trial, "All the physicians agreed that the murderer might have received little blood on his person, since its trajectory in both cases had been away from the direction in which the blows fell" (*A Private Disgrace*, p. 235). Medical examiner Dolan was satisfied that there was no spurting of blood from the wounds. It is a forensic fact related to me by an acquaintance who does volunteerism in the ER that the wounds that Andrew and Abby received do not always produce a great splattering of blood; in fact, sometimes there is very little or no splattering at all when death is instant. In the case of Andrew, any splattering seemed to land mostly on the ceiling and wall and not on the murderer. The same argument can be made for Abby's death, where most of the blood landed on either side of her and in front, but not in a backwards trajectory. This gives a powerful explanation for why Lizzie was found virtually stainless, although we know that the dress had been

45

slightly stained at least with paint, particularly at the hem, several months previously. But even if Lizzie did shield herself from blood-splatter, she could have worn one of the several rubber raincoats which were found in the closet at the top of the front staircase. If not a raincoat, she could have worn one of her father's coats which was inexplicably found tucked under his head at the crime scene. It has been theorized that Lizzie would have worn the coat back-to-front to ward off blood-spatter, but why the need? She could just as well have worn it in the normal way, buttoned up, and delivered her death-blows much more easily. Also, a big mysterious rolled-up blanket lay on the floor in the closet of Emma's room after the murders, but although the police spotted it, they didn't unravel and examine it. It was untidily rolled-up rather than neatly folded. Victorians were certainly not well-known for any high level of hygiene compared to our contemporary standards, but people of Lizzie's class were excessively neat and tidy people, and such blatant untidiness must have looked quite odd. To this day we don't know what was (or wasn't) in this bundle. That night, Lizzie went down into the cellar--first with Alice Russell and then a second time alone--and Officer Hyde who was guarding the house outside spied in through the cellar window and saw Lizzie stick something into the cupboard under the sink.

A very interesting thing happened on Sunday morning regarding the Bedford cord dress. Emma was washing dishes and didn't actually see her do it, but Lizzie took the cord out of a kitchen cupboard of all places! This cupboard was used only for kitchen utensils, so why on earth was the dress there? We don't know. What we do know is that Lizzie said, "I'm going to burn this old thing up, it is covered with paint". Emma said she insisted that she do it, and Alice Russell happened to walk in and witness Lizzie ripping parts of the dress up and burning them in the stove. It seems too much of a coincidence to believe that Lizzie burned that exact dress (which she had worn on the day of the murders) for an

Did Lizzie Borden Axe For It?

innocent reason. Yes, it was stained with paint--but given Lizzie's strange action it is reasonable to assume that it was somewhere also stained with blood and Lizzie realized that if it were put through close scientific examination, this would be borne out! She had just been told by Mayor Coughlin *the day before* that she was a suspect, and this must have scared her, so she wanted the incriminating dress destroyed. That is easily the most logical explanation for this mysterious act of dress-burning.

Lizzie said she was in the barn loft during the time when her father would have been murdered. But is this believable? The only witnesses who claimed that the barn was "cool" were two teenage troublemakers by the names of Brown and Barlow who were arrested for breaking into a store a few months after the Lizzie trial. The credibility of these juvenile delinquents' testimony is questionable at best, especially when compared to the statements of law-enforcement officers like Philip Harrington, Marshal Hilliard, John Fleet, and Patrick Doherty. Even Lizzie herself said that in the loft it was "very hot . . . close"! Yet we are expected to believe she spent 20-30 minutes in such excruciating discomfort by her own will? That's simply too hard to believe. I was once informed by Lizzie writer William Schley-Ulrich that his family had a similar barn as the one on the Borden property and he remembered as a boy how it felt inside there on humid summer days, that even 5 minutes under such conditions are too much to bear. On August 4, 1892 in Fall River it was a warm though not very hot day outside (only about 22 degrees Celsius), but there was high humidity without wind, and high up in the cramped quarters of the barn loft, with the door and windows shut and the air bad, and with the sun shining down on the roof with nothing to prevent its rays, one can imagine that the loft was much like a stuffy, boiling sauna in which the oxygen is sucked away. Lizzie could *not* have spent anywhere near 20 minutes up there as she claimed. If she went into the barn, and it seems that she did, as witnessed by Lubinsky, it was likely only a momentary visit. Officer Medley, who came onto the scene very early and was probably the first one up there, examined the loft and found no foot-prints in the thick dust. Another Lizzie lie. But there's more. What is even more interesting is that Lizzie claimed she went there for lead to make "sinkers" for an upcoming fishing excursion, and there was indeed a basket full of lead in the barn . . . *but* inexplicably she *didn't make* any "sinkers." If that was her reason for going to the barn, then why didn't she return to the house with her "sinkers"? The obvious answer is that her "sinkers" story was a lie, her weak alibi for her father's murder. In the same way her 9 o'clock "ironing" story was an alibi for her stepmother's murder. Her initial claim that she was looking for iron to fix a screen was also proven to be a lie when it was found that none of the screens in the house needed fixing. But that's not all, Lizzie just continued to trip over her ridiculously faulty alibi. She said she climbed up the ladder into the loft with 3 large pears (how she managed this without pockets and without three hands we shall never know) and ate them--4 pears in all if you count the one she said she had just eaten in the kitchen. These were not the smaller green variety of pear, but 4 big, brown pears. That's quite an appetite, Lizzie! . . . and perhaps a bit too much for us to swallow. Next she claimed that while up there eating her pears, she was looking out the window for almost the whole time and saw no one go in or out of the house during that brief and crucial span of time when a killer would have had to exit the side screen door, if he did in fact exist, because the cellar door and front door were locked. Yet no intruder or escaping assassin was seen by her or anyone at all on busy Second Street in front of the Borden house or Third Street behind it.

During the police searches that followed the murders, several hatchets and axes were found in the cellar. One of them in particular, known as the hoodoo hatchet or handleless hatchet, was presented at trial as the possible murder weapon. Its blade was found capable of inflicting all of the wounds, whereas the other axes and hatchets could only have produced some of the wounds. The handle had been sawn off, not broken off, and when the blade was examined the "cut" was found to be fresh and recent. There had been nothing wrong with the blade or handle, so why would somebody destroy a perfectly good hatchet like that by sawing the handle off? Would super-thrifty Andrew have allowed such senseless destruction? This makes no sense. It is incredible that Lizzie was never questioned about this hatchet. Furthermore, in the barn there was a vise and several saws which could have been used to cut off the handle, and in the cellar there was coarse coal ash from the furnace which had been found smeared all over the hatchet blade from *both* sides, as if the hatchet had been cleaned and then, perhaps wet, dipped in this ash to make it look like it couldn't have been used in the murders. Since there was no murder weapon at the crime scenes and the killer would not be expected to escape with the bloody murder weapon in broad daylight in a busy part of town, and because of the mysterious aspects of this handleless hatchet, it was believed by the police to be the murder weapon.

With regards to this hatchet, there is a very strange and overlooked story about it which is attributed to the maid Bridget on August the 18th and which puts Lizzie in a suspicious light. According to an official who was present at the inquest: "It was what Bridget saw, not what she heard, that led to Lizzie Borden's arrest. Bridget said she heard Lizzie down cellar hunting for something directly after Mr Borden went out to go down town and shortly after that she saw what she is positive was the hatchet lying half-hidden in the sitting room. She heard Lizzie down cellar before she went out doors to wash windows. She also saw the hatchet when she came inside to get some water to complete her work."

Lizzie is referred to by Morse's niece Henrietta as "peculiar"; Mrs. Cluny who once lived with the Bordens for a week as housekeeper, said "She was odd, very odd. I have heard a number of persons speak of it"; a store clerk referred to her as "surly"; at her inquest she put on a "haughty" air with Prosecutor Knowlton, and once when she didn't like the way a worker had laid bricks, she showed a ferocious temper with him (*Lizzie Borden: A Dance of Death*, p. 83). She was also known to be unforgiving, emotionally distant, "disagreeable", and her uncle Hiram Harrington, who Lizzie claims hated her father Andrew and would have nothing to do with her family, told the *Fall River Daily Globe* that "Lizzie is of a repellent disposition." George A. Pettey of Tiverton reported: "Lizzie is known to be ugly [unpleasant]." David S. Brigham, a former city marshal, said: "Lizzie Borden is known by a number of people to be a woman of bad disposition if they tell what they know." That's the kind of disposition that is consistent with crime.

A spot of blood, although only 1/16th of an inch in diameter, was found on Lizzie's white under-skirt a few inches from the hem. How it got there has never been satisfactorily explained because the stain was more apparent from the *outside* of the skirt than from the inside, therefore it couldn't have been from her "period". Laboratory tests were done and it was determined that the blood-spot matched all the characteristics of human blood. Also, Alice Russell testified about something very, very interesting (apart from the dress-burning) which I am amazed that the Prosecution didn't pursue further. She testified that when she saw Lizzie immediately after the murders in the kitchen where she was being comforted, she noticed that the blouse of Lizzie's dress "had pulled loose from the skirt in front, as it does when a woman lifts her arms to comb her hair or to reach something on a high shelf." Clearly, swinging a hatchet up and down could have put Lizzie's blouse in the same disarray.

And who can forget the Reagan story, which is one of the most intriguing and thought-provoking incidents in this whole saga? Hannah Reagan was a prison matron at Taunton Jail where Lizzie was detained for nine months pending her trial. She was on record as liking Lizzie, and she had no reason to make up a fake story against her.

Basically what happened is this: Hannah Reagan was tidying up Lizzie's cell on the morning of August 24, 1892 on the day before the preliminary hearing and her sister Emma came on one of her routine visits. Reagan went into the "toilet room" or dressing room so that the sisters could be alone, but then she heard "very loud talk" from Lizzie, so she came up to the door to look and listen. Lizzie was reclining on a sofa and Reagan saw Emma bending over Lizzie talking to her in subdued tones.

Suddenly Lizzie bolted and said, *"Emma, you have given me away, haven't you!"*

Emma replied, "No, Lizzie, I have not."

"You have," said Lizzie, "and I will let you see *I won't give in one inch!"*

Suddenly, Lizzie spotted Reagan by the doorway and she put her forefinger over her lips to Emma. They both fell silent. Lizzie turned over on the couch towards the window facing away from Emma, and the complete silence continued until Jennings came about two hours later. Hannah Reagan let him in.

Jennings must have noticed that something was wrong and he immediately asked Emma: "Have you told her all?"

"Yes, all," Emma replied.

Hannah Reagan revealed this incident to then-reporter Edwin Porter and soon it was in every newspaper reporting on the case. Incidentally, Porter would many years later write the first book on the case.

Understandably, this devastating account from Hannah Reagan made Andrew Jennings very nervous for his client and his pending legal case against the Prosecution, and he wrote up a statement for Reagan to sign saying that the whole incident was made-up. With Lizzie's closest devout defenders in tow--Rev. Buck and Marianna Holmes--he went back to the prison with the statement and it was decided that Rev. Buck would present it to

Reagan for her signature. Buck took it to her and said, "If you sign this paper, it will make everything all right between Miss Lizzie Borden and her sister."

Hannah Reagan replied that she would take it down to Marshal Hilliard and ask for his instruction on the matter. Rev. Buck said he would accompany her.

When Hilliard received and read the statement, he became very upset and dismissed both Reagan and Buck. He then thought through the matter and approached Reagan asking if her story was in fact true or not. She assured him that the incident between Lizzie and Emma had occured. Hilliard next went over to Jennings and gave him a piece of his mind about this illegal witness-tampering. Jennings was irate and left the prison waving his unsigned retraction statement and shouting at reporters stationed there: "This is an outrage! The Marshal has refused to let Mrs. Reagan sign this paper!"

But Jennings wasn't one to give up that easily, and he and Lizzie's inner-circle of arch-defenders continued to harass Hannah Reagan, pleading with her to sign the denial. There is no proof that Reagan caved in to them and made any denial, but it is likely that to appease them (as well as to get them off her back no doubt) she said something to the effect that she would have signed their statement if the Marshal had instructed her to. But Lizzie's arch-defenders twisted Reagan's words and went too far. On the witness stand, Lizzie's friends from church Charles & Marianna Holmes and her close friend from school-days Mary Brigham likely purgered themselves by claiming that Reagan said to them that the story was false and that she had wanted to sign the statement but that Marshal Hilliard had not allowed her to.

Hannah Reagan's trial testimony about this incident and her claim that it really happened is much more believable than Brigham's and the Holmes' biased claims. Reagan had no reason to "frame" Lizzie; but Lizzie's emotionally loyal friends had every

Did Lizzie Borden Axe For It?

reason to go to extraordinary lengths in her defense.

ANDREW J. JENNINGS.

Lizzie's family attorney, Andrew Jennings--courtesy Faye Musselman

Did Lizzie Borden Axe For It?

And last but not least, let's not lose view of the fact that Lizzie was and is the only obvious and plausible suspect--the only one. She had the motive, the opportunity, and the time--up to 20 minutes--to commit the last murder, hide the weapon away, and clean herself up, as argued in Paul Dennis Hoffman's *The Crucial 20 Minutes*. The murders were committed an hour and a half to two hours apart by most experts' calculations, so if it wasn't Lizzie, you have to believe that the murderer killed Abby and then waited over an hour in the house for Andrew to come home without knowing *when* Andrew would return--and he had to have the incredible luck and nerve to do this all completely undetected by Lizzie and Bridget. It is far easier to believe that Lizzie killed Abby a little after 9 o'clock after Abby had asked Bridget to go outside to do the windows, and then killed Andrew at around 11 when she saw Bridget finish with her work and go upstairs. As far as we know, Lizzie is the only one who had the opportunity to commit both murders; she was the first and last known person to see both victims alive.

Did Lizzie Borden Axe For It?

The facts against her are:

1) Lizzie had no consistent story for her whereabouts that morning.

2) She tried to buy poison four years before the murders--her reason being that she needed it to kill a cat. She allegedly chopped the head off of a cat in the basement. With her penchant for trying to obtain poison to kill an animal and swinging a hatchet to do the same, it's only one more step in a murderous mind to do the same to human beings--to the one she hates and to the other she feels betrayed by.

3) Lizzie was allegedly motivated by hatred of her step-mother and greed over her father's estate, as well as feeling a sense of resentment and betrayal that she thinks he prefers Abby. The hostility in the household was established by factual circumstances, like the unkind things Lizzie said about Abby, and the property on Ferry Street once belonging to their grandfather, which Lizzie/Emma demanded from Andrew because he had helped Abby financially to buy her half-sister a house on Fourth Street; the "girls" were furious that Andrew showed what they saw as favoritism towards Abby behind their backs. And *again*, just before the murders, Andrew was said to be doing something similar for Abby behind Lizzie's and Emma's back--he was getting ready to deed the property of Swansea to Abby.

4) Lizzie presented the Bengaline as the dress she wore that morning when everyone except the Bowens said she had on a different blue dress than the Bengaline--Mrs. Bowen especially was on record, according to one of the newspapers in *The Lizzie Borden Sourcebook*, as a strong and sentimental supporter of Lizzie's and her contradicted testimony about the dress may easily be explained away as biased in favor of Lizzie. The fact that Lizzie presented the wrong dress suggests emphatically that she was hiding the real dress because it had blood on it somewhere. That is the *only logical* conclusion, none other makes any logical sense.

5) Lizzie's claim that she was in the barn 20 or 30 minutes doesn't hold true when every witness except two dubious teenagers who are

otherwise known as "Me and Brownie" said that the barn loft was "extremely hot" and "suffocating", and that they "could hardly breathe" in there.

6) A potential murder weapon (the handleless hatchet) was found in the cellar as if disguised to look like it had not been used. Arguably, the reason an outside killer wasn't seen fleeing with a murder weapon is because the real weapon and the real murderer, Lizzie, never left the Borden property.

7) There are conflicting stories about Lizzie's personality and character--although there were pleasant aspects of kindness and generosity in her, some referred to Lizzie's dark side and described her in these exact terms: "peculiar", "haughty", "lazy", "surly", "unforgiving", "disagreeable", "repellent."

8) The blood-spot found on Lizzie did not appear to come from the inside of her under-skirt, that is, from her "period"; also, it was tested and found to be consistent with its possibly being of human origin. Also, the front of Lizzie's blouse was in loose disarray, and there has never been any explanation for this.

9) Hannah Reagan heard Lizzie's chilling prison cell-room confession: "Emma, you have given me away, haven't you . . . but I won't give in one inch!"

10) Lizzie is the only known person to have had the opportunity to commit the murders. Moreover, she arguably had just enough time to do it and clean up.

Works cited and/or consulted:
Eric Stedman, *The Borden Mystery Forum*, online website
The Superior Court Trial Transcript of the Lizzie Borden Murder Case, Vol. 1, pp. 1-988

Did Lizzie Borden Axe For It?

The Inquest Upon the Deaths of Andrew J. and Abby D. Borden, August 9 - 11, 1892, Volume I & II

Leonard Rebello, *Lizzie Borden: Past & Present*

Providence Evening Bulletin, January 17, 1969

Robert Sullivan, *Goodbye Lizzie Borden*

Victoria Lincoln, *A Private Disgrace: Lizzie Borden By Daylight*

Frank Spiering, *Lizzie*

The Commonwealth of Massachusetts vs. Lizzie A. Borden, The Knowlton Papers, Michael Martins and Dennis Binette, editors

New Bedford Evening Standard, November 22, 1892

Fall River Weekly News, October 11, 1893

David Kent and Robert A. Flynn, *The Lizzie Borden Sourcebook*

Agnes de Mille, *Lizzie Borden: A Dance of Death*

Fall River Daily Globe, August 6, 1892

Paul Dennis Hoffman, *The Crucial 20 Minutes: A Revised Lizzie Borden Timeline, Lizzie Borden Quarterly*, July 2001

Did Lizzie Borden Axe For It?

Conclusions

What are the conclusions to be drawn from all these various arguments for Lizzie's innocence and guilt? What has convinced you most? What do you believe happened? How did it happen? Who killed the Bordens? These are the questions. Except for the bare facts, the ones I have outlined near the beginning of this book, your guess is as good as mine about who committed these two homicides. We know that the victims probably weren't killed at around the same time, we know that there was tremendous cerebral damage inflicted--overkill is putting it mildly--and we know that the weapon was very sharp, with the length and shape of a blade that best resembles a hatchet rather than an axe or knife. But what happened to this hatchet and who swung it? We can only speculate.

However, there are clear facts that make some theories far more possible or probable than others. I have shown that a strong case can be argued both for Lizzie's innocence and her guilt. That's part of what makes this case so fascinating. It's not nearly as cut 'n' dry as so many other cases, which, though they may fascinate, lack its uniquely high mystery element. This case is far from solved, even though new facts and theories continue to pop up and be uncovered, some of them once regularly published in the *Lizzie Borden Quarterly*, a publication started by a man whose name all "insiders" know when it comes to Lizzie, Jules Ryckebusch, and then later published by another fine Lizzie scholar, Gabriela Adler. It was the only print publication in the world exclusively dedicated to the

Did Lizzie Borden Axe For It?

Lizzie Borden tragedy, first edited by Kenneth Souza, who was open to all viewpoints and ideas and didn't bar material from the quarterly, and then by Maynard F. Bertolet. Unfortunately, under its last editor the quarterly didn't fair as well, and presumably due to a declining subscription level and the printing costs, the publication has ceased.

What are the "obstacles" or "enemies" to solving this case? Subjective bias and the hiding or barring of evidence, ideas or information. Most regular people fascinated with this case are not in a position to hide or reveal any evidence, ideas or information to do with Bordenia, unless they are an author, publisher or editor. But subjectivity is the worm that continues to eat away at the apple of this case, if you will excuse the metaphor. Case in point: *Shattering the Myth* by Annette Holba which appeared in the July, 2003 issue of the LBQ. In his "editor's note", Bertolet erroneously referred to as an "intellectual" perspective what is really a scientific or psychological or perhaps pseudo-psychological perspective based on the theories and methods of a man named Kenneth Burke (1897-1993). When I did a study of this man's work and influence, he appears as a thinker of little renown compared to the other 20th century figures of thought in philosophy and psychiatry. In her quasi-objective article *Shattering The Myth* using Burke's ideas on rhetoric, Annette Holba basically tries to "shatter the myth" that there is any proof that Lizzie "did it"--she of course does this without admitting this is her intent. For example, she makes the assumption that the Fall River Police made the decision that Lizzie alone was their suspect as soon as Lizzie said that "Abby was not my mother, she was my step-mother"--when in fact the facts reveal that many suspects were seriously and pain-stakingly examined by the police for weeks and indeed even months after the murders. Unfortunately for her, based on circumstantial evidence, Lizzie appeared as the likeliest suspect out of them all, therefore she became the key suspect--nothing suspicious or unfair about that, just common-sense and common police procedure. If the police had not charged her, they may have been guilty of negligence. Then like some other works of Lizzie apologetics, the article explains away the inconsistencies of Lizzie's inquest testimony by saying she was drugged, not knowingly lying at all. As for Lizzie's strange little prussic acid episode, it is given no mention what-so-ever, as if it never happened. As for what Holba calls "hypothetical blood", that was no hypothesis--such a minute stain was found on Lizzie's undergarment, although there is more than one plausible explanation for it. Still, Holba's piece is perhaps the strongest defense of Lizzie yet written in essay or article form, a well-organized, well-thought-out, well-researched and well-written piece about motives that drove the actions surrounding the aftermath of the Borden murders, with its fundamental weakness being that it ignores all the circumstantial evidence against Lizzie, calling it "myth" and claiming that there is "no real link or direct evidence connecting Lizzie to the act of murder" without realizing that, while her claim is *technically* true, many murder trials involve suspects to whom the same applies, and yet often based on the overwhelming weight of circumstantial evidence they are found guilty in a court of law. In fact, the majority of murder cases are tried wholly on circumstantial evidence, not direct evidence or what is sometimes referred to as a "smoking gun."

The bias in Holba's "objective look" at the Lizzie Borden case is similar to the bias in Robert Sullivan's book *Goodbye Lizzie Borden*, except in his case the bias is *against* Lizzie, not for. The "camp" that views Lizzie as innocent includes the likes of Radin, Kent, Brown and Masterton. These writers use a blend of fact and theory to try to convince the reader that Lizzie was innocent and that there is another solution to the crime. They undervalue and under-evaluate facts that make Lizzie look like an unpleasant character or which point to her as the culprit. Their theories range from the believable and possible to the groundless and absurd. On the other

Did Lizzie Borden Axe For It?

hand, the "camp" that believes Lizzie guilty includes Porter, Pearson, Lincoln, and Sullivan. These writers consciously and/or subconsciously ignore or downplay evidence that points in Lizzie's favor. We particularly find this unfair bias in Victoria Lincoln's *A Private Disgrace*. More perniciously, this biased agenda appears in Edmund Pearson's *Trial of Lizzie Borden*, the most important early book on the case, yet flawed because it overlooks and deletes testimony and evidence that favors Lizzie. The authors from *both* "camps" make a crucial scholarly mistake. To them, it's either about a) trying to vilify Lizzie, or trying to vindicate her; to make her into an oddball "baddie" *or* to make her look like a sympathetic victim; b) trying to show that she committed the crime or trying to show that she didn't do the crime. Nevertheless, in response to the Holba article and its arguments, equally clever and effective arguments can be made to the contrary (see *The Question of an Outside Killer*). At the core of such bias is simply this: excluding and/or failing to mention things that contradict certain other facts or theories. Virtually all writers, to a greater or lesser degree, are guilty of this. "Complete objectivity" is, alas, an impossibility. However, it is possible for a writer to be as-objective-as-he-is-able, and in that case near-objectivity is possible. Even Len Rebello, known in Borden studies as the king of impartial bibliographical data-gathering, admits that he has theories and opinions on the case, even about who-dunnit, though he hasn't officially said what they are. But in fairness and in credit to Annette Holba's article, I quote the following from it, which is completely objective and completely true: "The [Lizzie Borden took an axe, etc] ditty is totally false. Line one: It was never proven that Lizzie committed the murders and no murder weapon was ever identified. Merely, the wounds are consistent with blunt force from a hatchet, which is not an axe. Line two: Abby Borden suffered approximately 11 wounds, not forty whacks. Line three: There is no immediacy involved in the crime. An hour and a half passed between murders. This line implies an immediacy which did not exist. Line four: Andrew Borden received between 18-21 wounds, not forty-one . . ." I agree that the ditty has always been used as a subtle piece of social "propaganda" against Lizzie and has simply "served a rhetorical purpose, to persuade people that Lizzie was guilty of the murders of her father and stepmother" when this has never been factually proven.

No one saw Lizzie do it, yet she must have? But Lizzie was downstairs ironing or in the barn looking for irons to fix a screen and lead to make "sinkers" for fishing (Lubinsky saw her with his own eyes coming from the barn), so how could she have been inside butchering her beloved father? Where could she find the time to clean up in such a short space of time? But then the other side can argue that she had a good 15 or 20 minutes from about 10:55 to 11:10 to clean up before she called down Bridget with the horrible news, and besides, it seems that she didn't get much blood on her at all, none that was noticed at least. Moreover, she had great trouble explaining where she was at different times that morning and unnerved poor Mr. Knowlton with her ever-changing account. But then one can pose a counter argument explaining this by saying she was emotionally befuddled and confused by Knowlton's lines of questioning (and Lizzie defenders will say she was drugged on morphine) and that that explains her confused testimony. And so on and so forth. This truly is the most complex, compelling, most fascinating murder case that I've ever come across, and I know of a good many. Until the day that humans cease to exist, there will always be the camp that proclaims Lizzie innocent in their hearts-- the Lizzie lovers, defenders, apologists; and there will always be the camp that condemns Lizzie as a vile murderess of members of her own family.

I could here give you my personal opinion about what happened. Perhaps I can even do it in such a convincing fashion as to make you change your previous position. But why should I do that? And what if I'm wrong? I might be leading you astray in that

Did Lizzie Borden Axe For It?

case, not that you'd ever know for sure with the mystery still unsolved and no sign of its ever *being* solved in our lifetime or any lifetime for that matter. Besides, what I personally think matters no more than what anyone else thinks about this question. We can debate, we can theorize, we can try to solve, but ultimately we're still in the dark. All we know is that she was acquitted at her trial by a 12-jury panel, and soon moved to a three-story, Queen Anne style home at 7 French Street, on "The Hill", which she named Maplecroft. Lizzie remains elusive. She teases us; she reveals herself in small new ways. But ultimately, she's an enigma. Still, we must keep peeling back the layers. We have a hunger, those of us interested in this case--we have a hunger to know more about her and about the facts and circumstances of this greatest of all mysteries. Our hunger is fed in small ways . . . but never fully satisfied . . . until the day we know *for sure* whether or not Lizzie Borden really took an "axe" and gave her parents 30 whacks.

Work cited and/or consulted:
Annette Holba, Shattering the Myth, *Lizzie Borden Quarterly*, July 2003

Did Lizzie Borden Axe For It?

II. The Private Lizzie

Lizzie Borden's unpublished diary, poetry and letters

Sharon Sexton's incredible story as related to me

In September of 2001, I had a most unusual (and that's putting it mildly!) correspondence with a woman named Sharon Sexton, formerly an amateur actress. She "played" a one-woman Lizzie show in Fall River, 1992 at the age of 42. She was then residing in a city nearby and is now domiciled in central Vermont. She changed her first name to Lizzie upon moving to Vermont because "my family had made a joke of my association with the Borden centennial." She resides with a woman friend (a widow), is divorced, and has a daughter in college. "I act as my friend's personal secretary, and caretaker as she has horses and travels a good deal . I have also performed with her but no longer . . . though she hosts the Art Song festival here and would have liked to have Lizzie Borden in full dress to entertain her friends . . . I refused. I lead a quiet life, Sir . . . I always did . . . even after the stage performances I indulged in I would never stay to greet theater goers as did the other performers . . . I'm quite shy about any talent I may have or not have . . . I never liked the limelight or the scrutiny, the possible criticism. My ego is fragile. The fact is Sir, I always suffered from very low self esteem and I have always been very self conscious about my looks. I did the stage work because I speak very well and the audiences seem to be able to feel my words . . . That was gratifying."

Here is Sharon Sexton's first letter to me, which certainly got my attention, as you can imagine:

"Dearest Sir~

In 1991 I was contacted by what has to remain an anonymous source and asked if I would be interested in representing Miss Borden interests. A well known forensic specialist [James Starrs], who obtained grant money by exhuming the famous/infamous dead was close to gaining approval to do the same to the Borden family. There was nothing to be gained by exhumation. My presence as Miss Borden in Fall River during 1992 was meant to raise public conscience. Lizbeth was no monster, no madwoman that suffered murderous "fits". She was wealthy in her own right before the tragedy of losing her parents and though she benefited by their deaths indirectly much of her money went to ongoing charitable causes. The stipulation that existed under my contract . . . I was never to deny nor admit the accusation that Lizzie murdered her parents. I was simply to say "I was acquitted". I was never to reveal the specifics of my contract, nor to divulge certain information gained through the resources I had at my disposal. I was given access to letters, diaries, tint types of family, pictures of friends and trips . . . her poetry . . . journals, personal items, etc . . . Though I was not allowed to use the personal items. I was only allowed to handle them.

Why was I chosen? I don't really know. There were many in my profession (acting) that might have done a better job of it. It will remain a mystery to me always and one I ponder often as my life took a strange path since that first day. . . . I still feel at times I am living her life. 1992 had a profound impact on my life. I will tell you honestly I never met the party(ies) that contracted me. Everything was delivered by a private messenger and returned by the same on a specific date set for retrieval. The journal, letters, cards, and gifts were retrieved by messenger at the end of January 1993.

This year I did a show with two friends of mine. . . . A professional soprano and classical pianist . . . it was something a bit different from their usual 'concert' as we incorporated poetry and I used Lizbeth, Lizzie as the character onstage to read it. I wrote the show and incorporated something in it about her personal life that I had agreed to divulge. It was subtle and I thought few would take it seriously but . . . before each performance I received a call. A digitalized voice that said "Ms. . . . You agreed never to reveal what you learned about Miss Borden. You are breaking a trust." I did the show three times for very small audiences and the calls so upset me that it triggered seizures onstage. (I am an epileptic). Needless to say I discontinued the show though I feel in my heart the time for 'that particular secret to come out' would hurt no one and perhaps help put ghosts to rest."

Naturally, I was intrigued, if not entirely believing of her story, and I wanted to hear more. Here was a woman claiming that Lizzie items (including poetry and a diary of Lizzie's) were lent to her from a private collection and that almost no one knows of these items. She claims she was "made to be Lizzie" in her private life during the time of rehearsals and production. The owner of the items remained anonymous and after a certain period collected the items back through "a messenger" who had delivered the items to her in the first place. Of course this is a bizarre story . . . but who's to say she didn't get to handle such items from a "private collection" which we may not be aware of?

Did Lizzie Borden Axe For It?

I wanted to know more and I asked her many questions. Here are some of her more interesting remarks (her words):

"I follow no quarterly, spoke to very few other than a Mr. Bernard Sullivan, editor of the newspaper in Fall River/1992 [Fall River Herald News] and the curator of the historical museum [Michael Martins] who warned me that Bernard Sullivan was 'in love' with Lizzie Borden and that I should take heed when I met him. . . . The curator I think will remember me. I know Mr. Sullivan and his wife. . . ."

"The incident of the gold ring . . . yes, you are correct [Lizzie gave Andrew her high school ring] . . . however only half that story was told. They exchanged rings. . . . He gave her a new ring that she had admired but thought not fitting what she considered were hands unbefitting a lady. She almost never wore it. It never fit properly and not at all as she grew older and heavier. She made a present of it to someone called Margaret. It was mentioned in her letter to cousin Grace.

"The items loaned to me came from an undisclosed source. No I don't think from anyone connected to the Fall River Historical Society as I was not treated as an expected guest there and I was paid in cash for my representation so there is no paper trail.

"Lizzie always felt 'mannish' less than feminine around women. It made her shy with them. She would write in her diary how she regretted certain incidences where she thought her comments were masculine or that she had laughed too loud (like a man). There was one afternoon in particular that stayed with her . . . a picnic with friends . . . a hillside with a shed that her companions felt marred the view. The conversation had been stilted due to the recent 'events' in her life and she thought a little humor might ease the awkwardness of talk . . . . She stood up impulsively, put her hands on her hips and shouted something like "bring me an axe, Tom", I don't recall the exact words she wrote . . . but there was a stunned silence and she knew immediately what her friends were thinking. . . . She hated herself for that comment and mulled it over in her mind many times during her life.

"There was no outside killer. I am almost positive. I can tell you that but will not and can not prove it. Only one person could . . . and didn't [an oblique reference to Emma?].

"I will also tell you Lizzie never lied and prided herself on it. It was a sort of game with her . . . not telling the whole truth either . . . even when it came to little things.

"Her Father was known as a hard business man but was not the penny pinching dictator that fed his family rotten stew as depicted in the movies and books. The family did have plans to move ... check the records. Andrew bid for a property but lost. A very well known piece of property in fact (smiling).

"Lizzie always considered herself rather plain though she did have beaus. One a teacher from Swanzee(sp) that used to meet her secretly despite his marriage. There is a picture of this teacher in a public collection. A group shot . Look for the dark rather homely man seated by a tree. The other man, the love of her life, a wealthy industrial foreigner; tall, blond and very handsome was involved with Nance though he met Lizzie secretly several times while she was abroad. He too was married and a ladies man." And later on: "The one thing they seemed to have [in] common was their secret selves and she wrote of it often to him (and he too agreed in the few letters he wrote). No pictures of this man exist in her collection. I traced the descendants of Lizzie's one true love and found a man. I had no knowledge of his background or anything much about him until 2 years ago when I started digging. . . .It was a shocking surprise to learn he was [allegedly] the great grandson of Lizzie's lover."

I began asking her specific questions. Who was this "Margaret" you refer to? What's in Lizzie's diary or journal? her poetry? Why did Emma really leave Maplecroft?

"'Margaret Streeter' [Sexton writes] is mentioned in two entries in the journal and a trip to 'take the waters' in New Hampshire. I don't know, but I think she was another performer (that Lizzie met through Nance?) who might have either met/traveled with them on this trip or was performing there. She had visited Lizzie and stayed with her at Maplecroft (there was mention of her being there at least once . . . but she is never mentioned again by name anywhere that I can remember). Margaret saw the ring in Lizzie's jewellery box, admired it greatly and Lizzie simply gave it to her. "I am foolish I know, she will only sell it. But what do I care? She can do as she pleases with it, I have several rings just like it," wrote Lizzie in her diary (quote).

"Emma inherited the estate of her deceased parents . . . not Lizzie . . . and though she distributed equally with her sister . . . she never let Lizzie forget her 'generosity' and whose money it was that Lizzie was spending when Lizzie decided to keep company with those of whom Emma did not approve.

"Emma could be cold and overbearing . . . a bit of a dictator though few in their circle of friends realized she had this other side. She always felt she knew what was best for Lizzie and her father. She assumed the role the first Mrs. Borden left vacant early on in life

69

and never let go.

"Concerning Lizzie's Journals. One for each year of her life . . . and in them described every thought, every feeling she had . . . concentrating mostly on the re-hashing of what she could have done, or had not done with the little time she had with her one true love. You see Mr. Rehak, he never loved her as she was not pretty enough (at least that's how she interpreted it). He actually told her that once. She went over and over what she perceived as her shortcomings in his eyes and her "ugliness". She was [a] very lonely, empty woman even in a crowd as all she ever thought about was this man. He entered into her thoughts every day of her life . . . right to the end.

"Concerning her poetry: Almost 90% of it was about love, longing and disillusionment.

"You ask about Nance. . . . She was a creature that reveled in her own beauty and enjoyed the attentions of both men and women, but though she would flirt and foreplay shamelessly with either sex if they indicated a physical interest in her . . . she was heterosexual. It was a game, sir that she did not, did not take seriously.

"About Nance in Lizzie's Diary: I am laughing again. Nance had an embarrassing habit of describing in detail her sexual exploits . . . which she shared often with Lizzie . . . they often provoked and awakened Lizzie's passion. . . . Lizzie I think was a bit of a voyeur . . . and her imagination, her dreams did on occasion create lively scenes, vivid scenes of watching others making love (not only the sexual act but rather the caressing, the pretty words, the kissing). She seemed to enjoy sharing these fantasies with Nance as she could without reprisal, and Nance sometimes, if it amused her, encouraged Lizzie. Many of Lizzie's entries concerning Nance though did end with Nance's 'needs' for financial support . . . which Lizzie always indulged. They are more of a postscript.

"Emma wanted out of Maplecroft and Lizzie's insistence to 'live' her life without the approval of friends, church and public caused many arguments. Lizzie also had an eye for beautiful expensive furnishings. This too was giving the wrong impression, Emma felt . . . attracting the wrong kind of attention. Yes, Emma left because of Lizzie's new found friends but it was not the *only* cause. Nance was an actress . . . one of many performers Lizzie would have round to Maplecroft. Unacceptable company for a woman in her position and . . . these people smoked and drank. That was the last straw. Lizzie wanted to explore her sexuality . . . Emma wanted to retire into the shadows of life . . . as was expected by Church, friends, and the public. Emma became very religious after the murders and close friends with Reverend Buck's daughter Alice, who had been a personal friend of Lizzie but started to shun her after she moved to Maplecroft. Lizzie didn't like Alice's strict religiosity and its influence over Emma, although Lizzie remained religious in her own way all her life.

"One notable entry in Lizzie's Journal . . . not an isolated one but notable. Emma's fear. She was uncomfortable with strangers in the house. Yes, after the murders Emma always kept locked all doors and at night had trouble sleeping. Often getting up to check if the entries had been secured. She feared that someone would hurt Lizzie as revenge for the acquittal. There were incidents where kids would knock on the front door and then run, and people would trespass onto the property uninvited. Once even a ground-floor window was pelted with eggs. Emma was increasingly fearful of going out in public. It became an obsession that would destroy her mind over the years. One night there was a small party. Emma came down and ordered everyone out of the house. Lizzie was embarrassed and told Emma to go back to bed. Emma said (not a quote but close): '*Do as*

Did Lizzie Borden Axe For It?

you are told, get those people out of here' . . . Lizzie reached for Emma's arm . . . wanting to talk privately and Emma slapped her for the first time (in the face) and shouted. 'Don't you think I know what you're up to!? You want me dead so you can do as you please!' A great shouting match commences. In the journal Lizzie writes that her sister is not herself since the murders and does not seem to be recovering from the shock. She ends with the comment 'my little mother is nomore' (quote).

"Dearest David ~ . . .
"I am smiling . . . you are a man that knows how to charm a woman . . . that is evident in your flattery of my small talent. However, my representation of Lizzie was not well received in Fall River by those intimately involved in the creation of the 1992 centennial. I tell you, again . . . this to warn you, Sir, whatever I have confided to you will be useless and should you pursue the truth behind the real 'Lizzie' you will become an outsider, mocked and ridiculed by those "experts" in the Borden case . . . and needless to say, sir . . . you will uncover no hard evidence that will prove she was innocent or guilty either if an end to this mystery is your goal. Of that I am quite positive.

"I am the only known source of this information. My past alliance with those who contracted me though legally was at an end after 1996. But it is in their mind a lifelong binding contract.

"I will never admit publicly that these remembrances came from me and will say that my letters to you were fiction should you publish any information that can [be] linked, or traced to me. 'They' will support me I am quite sure. They will undermine you unless you do by some miracle come up with evidence that reveals the killer's identity.

Did Lizzie Borden Axe For It?

"One other thing Dave . . .

I was not in anyone's mind ever the 'best Lizzie', though many may remember me. And please Dave . . . do not refer to Nance as a 'Sexy Amazon' . . . she was an exquisite ladylike vamp, fragile, soft, feminine in every way not an aggressive animal with a man's temperament as your description might imply."

Did Lizzie Borden Axe For It?

The Mystery That Was Lizzie

"People always say: 'The pure and simple truth of the matter is . . .'
But the [whole] truth is rarely pure, and never simple."
--Oscar Wilde

Her name was Lizzie "Drew" Borden, or Elizabeth Andrew Borden, or Lizbeth of Maplecroft, or Lizzie A. Borden, or just plain Lizzie: take your pick; she was known in life under all these slight variations, and in death she is Lisbeth *Andrews* Borden, as that is the name written on the family tomb.

In a fascinating article, Jules Ryckebusch looks back to his early days as a professor in the 1960's and points out that "At that time there were lots of people living in Fall River who had seen and talked to Lizzie, or who knew people who had worked for her or dealt with her in other ways. My students wrote more and better stories about Lizzie than any other topic I assigned, and their friends and families got involved. One student, whose mother worked for the Fall River School Department, brought to the class Lizzie's academic record from Fall River High School . . . We all learned that Lizzie was a below-average student who did not graduate. Another student, whose father was a Lieutenant at the police department, came to class one day with a set of the original police photos of the crime scene. His father had made the prints from the original negatives. It seemed as if everyone had some direct or indirect Lizzie connection. Students' parents and grandparents would write out anecdotes to bring to class. I truly regret not having done an oral history at the time. While most of the tales and remembrances could never be confirmed, there was alive in Fall River an awareness and some real knowledge of Lizzie . . ." Well, as he goes on to say, there is very little of that left here in our 21st century.

Today, it is extremely difficult and next-to-impossible to find living people who even remotely "knew" Lizzie to get their personal impressions of her personality and character, but I did interview a few such people, all of whom were small children at the time that Lizzie still lived. To my surprise, they all without exception referred to Lizzie as the most saintly and angelic kind of human being they had ever met. The model granny type. However, they had little to add that we don't already know from other sources, except perhaps that Lizzie liked to read or doze on her outside porch and to give certain children who knew her candies and sweets; she also let them play childish games like hide-and-seek in her house or tag in the big yard, which is reminiscent of the well-known factual account we have of a younger Lizzie allowing children to pick fruit from the yard of the Second Street property in the years before the murders. It's easier to find second and third hand accounts about Lizzie Borden passed down to newer generations; of course, these can be iffy and one is never 100% certain of their authenticity. Through some helpful networking, I also located and interviewed a retired gentleman named Trevor Fess who told me that many years ago in Brockton he had befriended a co-worker and former resident of Fall River who he remembers simply as "Cal" and who he only knew by acquaintance from the real estate agency where they both worked, but who related to him and the other employees that "I was a good friend of Lizzie Borden in my teens and early twenties until she died." When asked to expound on this, the man supposedly confessed some extraordinary things, including, as Fess recalls: "He said that he would take the train over to see Lizzie when he could

Did Lizzie Borden Axe For It?

get away from his studies. You see, he claims that Lizzie was friends with his mother and that Lizzie paid his college tuition. She was always very glad to see him and seemed to be eager for company. He said that what struck him was that her house was a bit plain and modest on the outside but really lavish within; Lizzie loved nice things, antique things. There was a part of him that felt very deeply sorry for her for the way she was treated by the snobbish and self-righteous hypocrites, as he referred to most of her neighbors and nearby residents. He was most emphatic about Lizzie being a very sweet, very gentle, very caring, very-very generous old woman who gave her chauffeur Ernie a big loan to buy his own house and was always compulsively doing some good little deed to keep herself occupied. She gave the library a lot of money too and bought many books from local book-shops to give to the poor. He said Lizzie was a voracious reader."

Postcard of the public library in Fall River of which Lizzie was a frequent patron

Did Lizzie Borden Axe For It?

It has also been confirmed for me by Lizzie playwright and scholar Carolyn Gage that Lizzie "was a generous donor to a variety of causes. She had stayed in touch with her high school teachers, and would pass along tickets for lectures and concerts to be given anonymously to deserving students. She paid all the medical bills for a retired former teacher in need of an operation, and later she paid the funeral expenses of this woman's mother. When a friend of hers lost a son and became too depressed to leave the house, Lizzie [temporarily] moved in with her, coaxing her back into the world."

It appears that there were two mysteries surrounding Lizzie: first, of course, the question of whether or not she committed the murders; but secondly, who was she? Who was Lizzie Borden really, deep down inside. There are conflicting opinions about her and many of them are more or less plausible, revealing different sides to her nature. Was she the brutal slayer of her own parents (a stepmother is still technically a mother, with a mother's role), or was she a kind, generous, innocent woman who happened to be in the wrong place at the wrong time and was lucky not to get killed herself? The majority of intelligent and informed minds, as long as they were not swayed by emotional bias for Lizzie, have for the most part decided that the likeliest scenario is that she was responsible for the murders or in the very least had an accomplice, and most opinion poles are unanimous in their belief about this and that she likely did the murders herself. If this is true, how does one reconcile the image of "Lizzie the killer" with "Lizzie the really nice person"?

To truly understand Lizzie, we must first understand that she wasn't an angel or the devil; she wasn't all black and white, she was shades of grey, a complex and paradoxical mix of bad *and* good, and the many accounts of her kindness and generosity bear this out, evening the scales against the accounts of Lizzie's more disagreeable personality traits. Yes, Judge Josiah C. Blaisdell, who presided over the inquest and preliminary hearing, was likely

Did Lizzie Borden Axe For It?

correct to find Lizzie "probably guilty" and set a date for her to appear before the Grand Jury. Though he was attacked by the newspapers, Blaisdell showed good judgment, given Lizzie's conflicting, self-incriminating inquest testimony and the testimony of Eli Bence, a clerk who remembered Lizzie trying to buy prussic acid, a poison, on the day before the murders. However, both of these testimonies were deemed inadmissible at the trial. Certainly if Lizzie was guilty of the murders, she deserved life in prison if not the hangman's rope, but she *was* a human being, same as us, with the same capacity for good and evil. She was capable of goodness, yes. Was she a kleptomaniac killer of her own parents? One could make an effective argument. But she was also known before the murders for her "many acts of kindness" when she worked for groups like The Young People's Society of Christian Endeavor or the Ladies' Fruit and Flower Mission, and it is almost impossible not to be touched and amused by the charming account of how she allowed poor kids access to the Borden yard to pick pears (*Lizzie Borden: The Untold Story*, pp. 46-47; see also pp. 50-52). Furthermore, after the murders her virtue continued only to increase, and she willed a whole mother-load of moola to the Animal Rescue League of Fall River to help poor little puppies 'n' kitties, she was also a great giver of gifts, she was capable of deep compassion and generosity towards friends and strangers alike, and more than a few times opened up her purse to them--these things we *do* know for a fact, as they are on record. How to reconcile these two completely opposing sides of Lizzie? I can't. Perhaps none of us can. It's the strange enigma and intriguing phenomenon that is Lizzie Borden.

Did Lizzie Borden Axe For It?

Works cited and/or consulted:
Edward D. Radin, *Lizzie Borden: The Untold Story*
Carolyn Gage, *The Real Mystery Behind The Fall River Murders,
feminista!*, Volume 4, Number 1
Jules Ryckebusch, Ah Yes! I Remember It Well, *Lizzie Borden
Quarterly*, April 2003
Gary Boyd Roberts, *Notable Kin*, Vol. 2

Did Lizzie Borden Axe For It?

Why Does Lizzie Linger?

During the Borden trial, Julian Ralph writing for the New York *Sun* predicted with astounding accuracy that "the Borden case will pass into history as one of the most mysterious of the celebrated cases of the century."

Why does the saga of Lizzie Borden go on and on and on and on? Why is there never an end? Why is there never a solution, a resolution to the crimes with the true killer truly identified and everyone lives happily ever after? But not only does the case refuse to be solved, Lizzie refuses to go away; in death, as in life, Lizzie refuses to move away from Fall River. I'm particularly interested in *why* Lizzie is such a uniquely fascinating case that continues to linger on and on while so many other once-renowned Victorian murder cases were front-page news and gripping beyond words at the time, but then died down and fell into obscurity. What are the things, point by point, that give the Borden case its "staying power" and keep us hooked on Lizzie and keep the facts & legends alive generation after generation? What makes Lizzie remembered and so many others forgotten?

First there are the essential ingredients necessary to make this story fascinating: a woman of unblemished reputation accused of the most hideous crime imaginable; a sizeable fortune up for grabs; Lizzie's very credible and impenetrable alibi and defense, yet how could anyone else have done the crimes and gotten away in broad daylight along a busy part of town?

80

Did Lizzie Borden Axe For It?

There is yet a somewhat more complex and sinister reason that Lizzie captivates and even attracts. There are some people who, while believing Lizzie guilty, wish they were able to act out in similar violent fashion against the people or things that bind or enrage them in their personal lives. Likewise, there are others, also believing Lizzie guilty, who feel that it is their ethical mission to prove or convince others that Lizzie "did it." Of those who believe Lizzie innocent, there are those who sympathize with or are "in love" with Lizzie and admire her as a hero or idol of sorts. Such people see aspects of themselves in Lizzie; for example, women who, like Lizzie, aren't especially pretty or enviable in their personal social lives but see in Lizzie a woman just like them who did so well for herself, regardless of whether she "did it" or not. Likewise, in this same group, there are also those people who, believing Lizzie innocent, genuinely think that she was telling the truth, if not absolutely than more or less, and that she was not guilty of the actual murders due to all the evidence that points in her favor. The Lizzie Borden case has *all* of the key ingredients for a great crime story, where almost all other cases have only one or some:

1) a large inheritance;
2) a suspect of perfect reputation accused of the most serious offence known to man;
3) no direct evidence against the suspect, although a mountain of circumstantial facts pointing at her;
4) profound sense of fascination with the person (some people see Lizzie as a symbol of aspects of themselves and their impulses; others see Lizzie as symbolic of evil and gross injustice).

Did Lizzie Borden Axe For It?

Lizzie As A Romantic Being

Lizzie Borden was a romantic woman, though she herself was lonely and unloved. Never had a suitor--at least in the conventional sense--that we know of; never knew the kiss of a man; never experienced a man inside of her deepest being, piercing her to the depths of her heart, soul, sex . . . or did she?

Like many women today, Lizzie liked a good cheap sentimental romance novel; but her tastes weren't confined to that. She also knew how to enjoy "serious" literature, including Carlyle, Emerson or Dickens, among her known favorites.

As a teenager, "Lizzie had crushes on school teachers that she talked about freely" and she is alleged to have been "sentimental, and sexually immature" (*A Private Disgrace*, p. 294). Her teachers described Lizzie as an average student at best, not stupid but not especially smart or dedicated either, and due to a lack of interest, she dropped out of high school in her "junior year" and for the next ten years lived a very uneventful and reclusive life at the Borden house. She was never in need of friends, but although she attended social functions and was occasionally driven around and escorted by men, no man ever seemed to take a truly serious interest in her, except perhaps an itinerant preacher named Curtis I. Piece (or Pierce) when she was in her early twenties. Many years later, he had been out of touch with Lizzie at the time of the murders in 1892, but he wrote to Lizzie's lawyer and prison matron, asking and almost pleading for permission to see Lizzie at Taunton jail to speak with her, assuring them of his sympathy. But Pierce's request was denied, and her lawyer Andrew Jennings replied that Lizzie didn't want to see him because of his "previous conduct" towards her. What was this "previous conduct"? What did he do to fall out of favor with Lizzie? We know nothing, Jennings doesn't say. According to the *New York Herald*, "she never had a lover, she has avoided the company of young men." Nevertheless, there were a few rather spicy rumors. Doctor Seabury Bowen from across the street started accompanying Lizzie to church when she began to attend in her late-twenties. They were seen arriving in a buggy together and this had the gossips wagging their tongues, especially when they saw them sitting together in the pews. Page 21 of the *Witness Statements* states, according to one Jane B. (Negus) Gray, who lived on 188 1/2 Second Street in 1892 and who according to Paul Dennis Hoffman was called as a witness at the trial but did not testify: "Four years ago, while the Borden family were summering over the [Taunton] river on the [Swansea] farm, Lizzie remained at home. One Sunday evening during this time, she and Dr. Bowen came to church together, and sat in the Borden seat. I myself saw them this evening. At the time, and since, there was much comment on this act. Some remarked how courageous she was to remain in the house alone; but others replied in a knowing way, perhaps she has very acceptable company." [hint, hint!]

It may also be pointed out that according to an unidentified Borden relative, allegedly there was incest between Lizzie and Uncle John V. Morse. This has not been proven to my knowledge. As well, it was implied by Fall River police at the time that there was "undue familiarity between Lizzie and her uncle [John Morse]" (*Lizzie Borden, Past & Present*, pp. 134-35). In the *Fall River Herald* following the murders, one reads: "There is always a skeleton in most houses, and the home of Mr. Borden's was no exception. By members of the family it was known that *Lizzie regarded Mr. Morse with more tenderness than most nieces feel*

Did Lizzie Borden Axe For It?

for their uncles. This Mr. Borden was aware of, and he was constantly on the alert to see that the breath of scandal did not reach his home." In fact, Morse had had a reputation as quite a ladies' man. It was also rumored that he had his eye on Bridget, although this has never been substantiated. On previous visits, he did however sleep in the attic room beside Bridget's. Whether there was really any "hanky-panky" involving him and his niece Lizzie or the servant-girl Bridget we will never know. Anyway, the theory that Lizzie may have been a victim of or wilful participant in incest is an old one, and well-argued by Marcia R. Carlisle's *What Made Lizzie Borden Kill?* and Eileen McNamara's *Psychological Profile: Was Lizzie Borden a Victim of Incest?* For days before the funeral, the bodies of Andrew and Abby were laid out on the dining-room table. In a spontaneous gesture, at one point Lizzie bent down and lovingly kissed her father's mutilated face with compassionate tears in her eyes, like the kiss of a devastated, heartbroken lover. I'm reminded of the famous verse: "All men kill the thing they love; some do it with a kiss, and others with a sword."

Still, there is no conclusive evidence that Lizzie participated or was made to participate in incestuous acts with her father Andrew or uncle Morse. As for Pierce, the *Witness Statements* on page 34 claim that Lizzie had found him to be intolerable (according to Lizzie's close friend Augusta Tripp); Bowen too was out of bounds for her, he was a married man and many years older. It is quite probable that Lizzie would have liked to have indulged in her romantic side if she could, but it appears she had no opportunity (at least in the conventional sense), so instead, she read in the papers about the dances, parties, dinners, courtships, engagements, and weddings of the upper crust, which in Fall River meant the people living on "The North Hill," and fantasized about being a part of it all; also, of course, she read the romantic novels of the day and lost herself in a world of dashing young men who sweep their beautiful heroines off their feet.

Did Lizzie Borden Axe For It?

Lizzie not long before the time of the murders. She is generally not believed to have been a very pretty woman, but this is probably her most attractive photograph

Did Lizzie Borden Axe For It?

Lizzie with pince-nez in the early 1900's

Did Lizzie Borden Axe For It?

In middle age, Lizzie became infatuated with the stunningly talented American actress Nance O'Neil and sought her out. They quickly became friends and Lizzie was invited to her summer home in Tyngsboro. In time, rumors spread that the relationship was indeed a romance, especially since insiders were aware that it was a well-known though unmentionable and unprintable secret that Nance O'Neil had lovers of both sexes. It is said that there are letters to prove it, although I haven't been able to track them down. Anyway, apparently, the conservative Emma did not approve of the "friendship". It seems likely that it contributed to Emma's leaving in 1905, since Lizzie's "inseparable" 2-year relationship with Nance lasted from 1904-1906. Nance O'Neil is reported to have had many lovers and admirers in her lifetime, and she described her "fling" (if that's what it was) with Lizzie as brief, though unforgettable. According to the *New Bedford Standard*, clearly Lizzie made an impression on Nance, who found "her gray eyes and graying hair and her unmistakable air of refinement and intellect, distinctly attractive." In this same phase of her life, Lizzie had hired a handsome young coachman named Joseph Tetrault or Tatro in 1899. He was employed by Emma and Lizzie Borden from 1899-1902 and 1904-1908. When Emma left Lizzie in 1905, newspapers reported that Emma Borden did not like Mr. Tetrault nor his "doings or position as coachman . . ." He was later rehired as coachman and remained at French Street [Maplecroft] until 1908. "Miss Emma is said to have found offense in his comfortable preferment. Tetrault was a fine looking young man and reported to be very popular with the ladies, although Miss Emma took a dislike to him." Faye Musselman, a very knowledgeable scholar of the case has stated the belief that Lizzie and her coachman Joseph Tetrault may have been lovers. So, with Lizzie bed-hopping from Nance to Joseph and then back again, we can indeed imagine just how the

Did Lizzie Borden Axe For It?

very Victorian Emma would have eventually said enough's enough

and moved out.

In 1896, according to the *Fall River Herald News* and the *Fall River Daily Globe* of December 10, it was reported that Lizzie was shortly to marry a Mr. Gardner, who supposedly lived in Swansea a few miles away across the bay. Further research reveals to me that this "mystery man" really existed and was indeed a teacher from Swansea. Sherry Chapman brought my attention to the fact that his name in all probability was Orrin A. Gardner (1867-1944), a cousin of Lizzie and Emma, and a school teacher or principal by profession, according to *Yesterday In Old Fall River*, p. 135. The *Boston Globe* of the same day quickly picked up on the story and reported that the wedding was set for Christmas-time. There were many Gardners living in Swansea village at the time, but is this the school teacher from Swansea that Sharon Sexton claims was Lizzie's secret lover? Lizzie started getting congratulatory letters from all over the country from friends and strangers alike, but she hastily denied the rumor, as she certainly would have had to if he was already a married man, which is what Sexton states. He had apparently known Lizzie since childhood when she would accompany her father to the Swansea "farms" as a young girl; the Gardners lived at the farm next to Andrew Borden's. The man in question was the Gardners' son who had just built a house in South Somerset. It was he who was rumored to be Lizzie's secret love. When the story of the affair broke out, he fled town until the excitement died down. Lizzie meanwhile stood her ground and did and said anything she could to deny the embarrassing allegation, writing letters to the likes of the bridal dressmaker Cummings and telling reporters that the whole thing was a lie. Lizzie no longer had any openly known connection or association with Orrin Gardner after this, but mysteriously, Emma Borden left him ten thousand dollars in her will, a very considerable sum in those days. Why would she do such a thing? Did she do it for Lizzie because Lizzie couldn't make such a gesture in her own will without arousing suspicion? Sherry Chapman tells me that "some speculated that the newspaper publicity made Gardner shy away from Lizzie or that she did not want to submit him to the inevitable negative public exposure. Others believed that the entire story was simply fabricated." Did Lizzie have an affair with this man? Although it is generally believed to be merely a rumor, the Gardner story has never been satisfactorily disproven. It was simply denied by Lizzie, and Lizzie writers have simply taken her word for it. But the Fall *River Herald News* was a very reputable newspaper which, unlike the *Boston Globe*, did not engage in yellow journalism and was known to meticulously check out the authenticity of its news sources before printing their stories. Given this and other factors, the rumor seems far less iffy than may have appeared previously. Indeed, there are times when so-called rumors turn out to be true.

Long after Lizzie's death, in 1984 a retired nurse in her old age named Ruby Cameron who claimed to have looked after Lizzie in Fall River's Truesdale Hospital in 1926 when she was having problems with her gallbladder, said that Lizzie confessed to her that "her boyfriend David Anthony" had committed the crimes. The man's identity was discovered (he had died in 1924), but if he was indeed responsible for the murders, Anthony would have been only around 22 years of age at the time, while Lizzie was 32. This story, though intriguing, has nothing whatsoever to support it.

Did Lizzie ever know the lover's touch? So far all we have is rumor and conjecture. Victoria Lincoln, at least, wrote that she believed that Lizzie was incapable of a love-affair. Lizzie's unmarried sister Emma almost certainly died a virgin, as there was never so much as even a rumor about her having a love-life; Lizzie, as far as we know, died fully "intact" as well. A lonely spinster with dreams of love . . . but only dreams. Or . . . ?

Did Lizzie Borden Axe For It?

The summer home at Swansea in the days when Lizzie owned it

Did Lizzie Borden Axe For It?

TRUESDALE HOSPITAL, FALL RIVER, MASS.

91545

Postcard of Truesdale Hospital in the 1920's where Lizzie was a patient under an assumed name and underwent a gallbladder operation in 1926

Did Lizzie Borden Axe For It?

Works cited and/or consulted:

Marcia R. Carlisle, What Made Lizzie Borden Kill? *American Heritage*, July / August, 1992

Eileen McNamara, Psychological Profiles: Was Lizzie Borden a Victim of Incest? *Lizzie Borden Quarterly*, April 1993

The Witness Statements For The Lizzie Borden Murder Case

Fall River Daily Globe, December 10, 1896

Boston Globe, December 10, 1896

Boston Herald, June 3, 1905

New York Herald, August 5 and 6, 1892

Victoria Lincoln, *A Private Disgrace: Lizzie Borden By Daylight*

Edward D. Radin, *Lizzie Borden: The Untold Story*

New Bedford Standard, June 4, 1927

David Kent and Robert A. Flynn, *The Lizzie Borden Sourcebook*

Leonard Rebello, *Lizzie Borden: Past & Present*

Paul Dennis Hoffman, *Yesterday In Old Fall River: A Lizzie Borden Companion*

Did Lizzie Borden Axe For It?

Was Lizzie A Lezzie?

"I did not realize that what is whispered in the private bedchamber
would one day be shouted from the rooftops"
--Oscar Wilde

"In the course of her trips to Boston, Lizzie went backstage to make
the acquaintance of the actress Nance O'Neil. Miss O'Neil had seen
better days on the stage, but the tragic roles she typically played
struck a chord with Lizzie. After they met backstage, Lizzie invited
Nance O'Neil, and some others of the theater set, to Maplecroft for a
catered party, complete with live music and drinks all around. Poor
Emma, ever the prim and proper elder sister, could no longer abide
Lizbeth's behavior. She was consorting with an immoral lot and
showing no shame about it. Emma moved out. Though they had
been through a great deal together, to say the least, the two sisters
never spoke again. The old Women's Christian Temperance Union
and churchgoing set, once Lizzie's staunchest defenders, now joined
Emma in their embarrassment over Lizzie. Some of the Puritan
gossip centered on Lizzie's sex life, including the theory that she and
Miss O'Neil were more than mere friends" (*Gendered Justice:
Lizzie Borden and Victorian America*, pp. 60-61).

Lizzie's alleged romance with Nance O'Neil was much
whispered about, but was Lizzie really bisexual or gay? We know
Nance O'Neil was known or suspected to be. Carolyn Gage refers
to her as an overt lesbian. In fact, Nance's supposed homosexuality

was so well-known in theatre circles that "the popular slang term for homosexuals became 'nance.' Al Jolson, who was a popular actor of the times, had a favorite offstage joke which involved this fictional exchange between two Shubert chorus boys:
FIRST BOY: "Do you know Nance O'Neil?"
SECOND BOY: "No. Who is he?"

This is an allusion to the common 19th century notion that lesbians were cross-dressers. Al Jolson's use of 'nance' mannerisms onstage led some contemporaries to question his orientation. Having the flamboyant 'Pansy' Holmes as his personal dresser only added to the groundless talk. But Jolson was decidedly heterosexual, and smart enough to know that a little backstage gossip would do him no harm."

But what about Lizzie? Was she ever known to have a female lover? Was she attracted to men? Even Joe Howard, a prominent journalist whose articles were pro-Lizzie, wrote that it was peculiar that "she never cared at all for the society of men, young or old." Let's examine the evidence. There is nothing whatsoever to suggest that Lizzie had lesbian consciousness or acted upon it while she lived at 92 Second Street. Theories about her and Bridget being lovers are not supported by anything. Ah, but what about her more "liberated" existence at Maplecroft? It is a fact on record that she enjoyed entertaining visiting friends. According to at least one source: "Lizzie Borden was reportedly a lesbian who held women's gatherings in her home during the years she lived there after her parents' murders."

In 1897, Lizzie wrote a letter to a lady "friend" that includes the words "*I dreamed of you* the other night *but I do not **dare** to put my dreams on paper*." The meaning of this passage seems obvious. It cannot be mistaken for a sentiment of friendship--it is clearly passionate or *romantic*. It was common in the Victorian age for women to express their friendship for each other in fervent ways that to our sex-sensitive age would come across as suggesting

Did Lizzie Borden Axe For It?

romantic feeling; phrases like "I love you" or "I adore you" and "you are the sweetest little thing" are common in such letters and their meaning may be non-sexual; but I have never come across a letter in which a woman tells her friend that she dreamed about her but doesn't dare tell her what it is unless it refers to sexual or romantic sentiments. Why wouldn't she *dare* put her dream on paper? One can only assume that the dream is amorously daring. What other explanation is there for her phrase, really. I would love to hear even *one* other good possible explanation for that phrase in Lizzie's letter, if there is one. Clearly, no other apparent explanation for it comes to mind. Unless you want to believe that she dreamed of killing her friend, and that's why she doesn't dare put her dream on paper! But all kidding aside... Incidentally, Eleanor Roosevelt, when she was a young woman at the turn-of-the-century, was much admired by the young ladies at Allenswood, an all-girl "finishing" school in England run by a highly sophisticated and emancipated free-thinking lesbian Frenchwoman named Madame Silvestre, and she received flowers and devoted love letters from her fellow student admirers who had "crushes" on her. Lizzie's letter to her "dear friend" concludes "I should be very glad to hear from you."

Jules Ryckebusch, a former professor at Bristol Community College (now retired) and prominent Lizzie scholar, believes in the lesbian theory (*Lizzie Borden: Past & Present*, p. 140). In Agnes deMille's *Lizzie Borden, a Dance of Death* we read the following: "William Trowbridge Forbes, Judge of Probate Court in Worchester County [Massachusetts], had a curious case at the turn of the century, of *a man divorcing his wife on charges of lesbianism. The co-respondent named in the proceeding was Miss Lizzie A. Borden of Fall River*. Judge Forbes dismissed the charges as frivolous . . ." (p. 84). Len Rebello informs me that this occurred in 1909, but that he is unable to verify the charges; one would have to have the man who filed the charges. Then on page 95 of de Mille's book comes an unverified story from a Hollywood actress from Fall

Did Lizzie Borden Axe For It?

River now buried in Oak Grove Cemetery named "Mrs. Otis Skinner; whom she had it from is not known. When Lizzie was living in her new home and maintaining what friendships were possible under her new circumstances, she read of the death of a schoolmate and immediately and considerately got in touch with the bereaved daughter and asked if there was anything she could do. Yes, it seems, there was. Apparently the daughter was without household help and wished to go shopping for some black things as the funeral was to be the next day. Would Miss Lizzie be kind enough to sit with the body? This request seemed perfectly congenial to Lizzie and she hurried over. The daughter shopped, returned to find all quiet in the death chamber, thanked Miss Lizzie and showed her out. Something, almost nothing, but some little disarray about the corpse prompted investigation. *The daughter had laid out Mama in her very best hand-sewn, lace-bordered underwear. The corpse was* **now, after Miss Lizzie's departure,** *quite naked under the outer garments.*" [note: Lizzie was known to steal things, and some believe her to have been a kleptomaniac because she did it even though she had the money to pay; see *Kleptomania and Incest*].

In 1915, the private publication of an autobiography by one Alicia Morris called *My Life: Loves, Happinesses and Sorrows* appeared. Morris purports to have been a friend of Annie Fields, who was a very close companion and, some believe, lover of the once well-known Massachusetts author Sarah Orne Jewett. In this autobiography for 1903? is the following tantalizing passage: "Annie [Fields], Miss Kowalski, Sarah [Jewett], and I spent an afternoon at the home of Lisbeth(sp) Borden, who was involved in a famous murder trial some ten years ago. She is a wonderful woman, much given to laughter and conversation. Those who call her melancholy or sad are mistaken. We had tea on the piazza [porch?]. When I told my husband that evening that I had been at the home of Lizzie Borden, he was quite indignant with me." Then later: "Sarah

Did Lizzie Borden Axe For It?

several times invited Lizzie [Borden] to the seaside cottage when Annie was away in Rhode Island to see her cousins. *I have often wondered if the sapphic dalliances of Lizzie which so infuriated her sister began there.*" [note: "sapphic" is an old-fashioned term for lesbian].

Sarah Orne Jewett, who was a famous Massachusetts author, suspected lesbian, and alleged lover of Lizzie Borden

Did Lizzie Borden Axe For It?

In *Surpassing the Love of Men*, we are told that Sarah Jewett never took a husband. She had a life-long relationship with the woman Annie Fields, who was the widow of prominent publisher James T. Fields. The two women lived together, what was then regionally commonly called a "Boston marriage." Literary scholars however don't like to see an author's personal life get more attention than their work because it's the work itself that's important, and although they concede that Jewett may very well have been homosexual or homosexually inclined, that kind of speculation distracts us from her writing.

The autobiography by Alicia Morris is allegedly mentioned by a Mary Boucher in one of her letters (a woman by this name worked as a maid for Lizzie), but I haven't been able to verify the information in those excerpts with any other sources. I must also admit that I have been unable to collaborate Agnes deMille's accounts with additional sources. But even given that, however, the case for lesbianism is still compelling.

There have been many books, some of them fiction and others non-fiction, exploring the possibility of Lizzie's alleged homosexuality, written by authors like Elizabeth Engstrom, Evan Hunter, Walter Satterthwait, Charles & Louise Samuels, Frank Spiering and Agnes deMille. It's obviously a popular notion and a tantalizing question.

Aside from lesbianism, which would have been consensual, there have also been hints that Lizzie was an incest survivor. "Her unnatural closeness to her father and sexual estrangement from all other men suggest the possibility of sexual abuse. Although it will never be known for sure, whispers of incest still linger behind the locked door of Andrew Borden's bedroom which is today part of the Lizzie Borden Bed and Breakfast." In fact, quite a number of modern psychiatric experts suspect sexual abuse/incest was at the heart of the murders. Some even argue that the almost fanatical outpouring of sympathy for Lizzie before and during her trial from certain people suggests that such individuals understood or even excused her crime, perhaps even "silently applauding her for doing what they could not do in their lives" but at the same time in their fear of public criticism "they could not publicly condone her by associating with her after the verdict." My own conversation with a psychology professor from my local university of Malaspina here in Nanaimo taught me that incestuous victimization sometimes leads to homosexual inclination in a person.

Edith C. Hart was a bookkeeper in Fall River, where she married and lived most of her life. At around the turn of the century she saw Lizzie on various occasions in public and was privy to all the lurid rumors about her, although she wasn't a close friend. Mrs. Hart is now deceased, but an aged relative of hers agreed to be interviewed, although prefers to remain anonymous. As a researcher gathering material and information on this murder case, I have discovered it is not altogether uncommon for some people to prefer to remain anonymous. Anyway, she told me: "Lizzie Borden as I understand it liked to travel quite a bit outside of Fall River on occasion, and got to know some influential folks. There was always gossip too. *Aunt Edith talked plenty [about] what she heard about Lizzie's havin' affairs with actresses and admirers and such.* Of course you couldn't read about that. But there was lots of wild word-of-mouth tales going round. Some people really hated her awful bitter. They thought she was capable of anything and guilty of anything--murder, adultery, incest, *homosexuality*, stealing, lying, you pretty well name it."

In conclusion, given the weight of the circumstantial evidence (the only real evidence possible in this sort of examination), and although it is still technically unproven, it can be strongly argued that Lizzie did find solace in the arms of a member(s) of her own sex. Perhaps it is yet another secret that she took with her to the grave.

Did Lizzie Borden Axe For It?

Works cited and/or consulted:
The American Experience: Eleanor Roosevelt, 2000, a PBS documentary
Our Love Is Here To Stay - Part III, 1900-1940: Life Upon The Wicked Stage, author unknown
Boston Globe, June 20, 1892
Featured Landscape Coin Drops, Month by Month, author unknown
Letter dated August 22, 1897, signed "Lizzie A. Borden."
Leonard Rebello, *Lizzie Borden, Past & Present*
Agnes deMille, *Lizzie Borden, A Dance of Death*
Evan Hunter, *Lizzie, A Novel*
Elizabeth Engstrom, *Lizzie Borden*
Walter Satterthwait, *Miss Lizzie*
Charles Samuels and Louise Samuels, *The Girl in the House of Hate*
Alicia Morris, *My Life: Loves, Happinesses and Sorrows*
Lillian Faderman, *Surpassing The Love of Men*
Dottie Webb, *Nineteenth-century Regional Writing In The United States*
Marjorie Dorfman, *Who Is Lizzie Borden?* PageWise, Inc
Irene Stuber, *Women's History Month Collection*, Episode 9, 2000
Walter L. Hixson, *Gendered Justice: Lizzie Borden and Victorian America*

Did Lizzie Borden Axe For It?

Kleptomania and Incest

In 1897, a firm of Jewellers by the name of Tilden and Thurber had a warrant for Lizzie's arrest, claiming that she had shoplifted "two small decorated pieces of porcelain bric-a-brac" (*Goodbye Lizzie Borden*, p. 208); the paintings were given by Lizzie to a lady friend (perhaps lover) and had an amorous motif, called *Love's Dream* and *Love's Awakening*. Tilden Thurber Co. had a well-established reputation and was renowned for over a century for its stylish art collections.

Lizzie paid a visit one autumn afternoon in 1896. Addie B. Smith was manager of the store at the time, and her knowledge of the customer's identity made her keep a watchful eye on her.

"Lizzie asked to see a vas, which Addie had to go to the back of the building to find. When she returned with it, Lizzie declared that it wouldn't do at all and strode hastily away.

"Lizzie had been alone on the floor.

"Before anyone else entered the gallery Addie Smith noticed that one large and one small porcelain painting were missing from the stand where they had been displayed. Addie also recalled that Lizzie had been wearing a voluminous fur coat.

"She immediately reported the matter to her employer, Mr. Henry Tilden.

"Tilden told her that there was nothing that could be done" (*Lizzie*, p. 191).

Then a few months later in early 1897, Addie Smith saw a

Did Lizzie Borden Axe For It?

woman enter the store who showed her a porcelain painting. Miss Smith immediately identified it by its size, shape and frame as one of the paintings that had disappeared along with Lizzie some five months earlier. The woman claimed that Lizzie Borden had bought her the painting for Christmas but that she had accidentally broken it. She wanted it fixed.

The Providence police was soon notified of the affair and Lizzie was officially charged with the theft of the two paintings, valued at less than one hundred dollars, from the Tilden-Thurber gallery.

The Tilden-Thurber building (today) from which Lizzie was alleged to have stolen--courtesy Faye Musselman

Did Lizzie Borden Axe For It?

But this wasn't the first time Lizzie was alleged to have stolen. "The petty thefts from Mrs. Borden's room, break-ins at the barn, now shoplifting--it all shows a pattern of compulsive stealing, or kleptomania. Often, the act of theft in cases of kleptomania substitutes for a forbidden sexual act--often incest (Gutheil, 467). Furthermore, Dr. Gutheil comments, 'It is not sufficiently known that behind kleptomania often a much more serious impulse may be hidden than that of sexual aggression: the impulse of murder (469).'" As a teenager, Lizzie lovingly gave her high school ring to her father and he never took it off, it was a symbol of their special bond. But if that bond was severed "by any overt or implied act of 'discourtesy' [or betrayal], it cost him and his complacent wife, Abby, their lives" (*Lizzie Borden Unlocked*).

As for the paintings, Lizzie was careful to resolve the dispute privately and out of court with the help of her lawyer Andrew Jennings, and the warrant was never served. Upon returning home and concluding the embarrassing affair, Jennings said: "I will have nothing to do with that woman."

Works cited and/or consulted:
Robert Sullivan, *Goodbye Lizzie Borden*
Victoria Lincoln, *A Private Disgrace: Lizzie Borden By Daylight*
Frank Spiering, *Lizzie*
Ed Sams, *Lizzie Borden Unlocked*
The Providence Daily Journal, February 16, 1897
Brockton Sunday Advertiser, September 13, 1992

Did Lizzie Borden Axe For It?

A 120-year-old Lady Reveals What She Remembers About Meeting Lizzie

Suella Sams apparently resides in a place called Seclusion Bend in Tennessee, though I personally have checked my atlas and been unable to locate the place. Small town? She is alive, remarkably, about 120 years of age, and lives with her nephew and an old cat. Suella graduated from Mars Hill College in 1911 and is a member of the Society for the Protection of the Snail Darter, Women's Auxiliary. Still in amazing control of her wits, she has an online column on an internet site called Yellow Tulip Press, which publishes and sells chapbooks on Oscar Wilde, Houdini, Queen Victoria and other fascinating historical figures.

Suella claims to have met Lizzie while she was in Taunton jail awaiting trial.

Her account which I read and made a record of some years ago from the website was as follows:

"In 1892, when the Fall River murders took place, I was merely a little lass. However, I did have the opportunity to see Miss Lizzie in the flesh (so to speak) when I was part of an inter-denominational foreign exchange program between church choirs from Tennessee and Massachusetts. As I recall, my fellow choristers and I were forced to use our folded parasols to poke our way through the enormous crowd of press gathered outside Miss Lizzie's jail cell. Once there, we entertained the prisoner with a hearty rendition of 'Throw Out the Lifeline,' only to be greeted by all manner of rebuff by the newspaper people. I believe it indicated a shocking lack of manners!" (*Ask Cousin Suella*).

I tried to contact her for further comment about this alleged incident and I was interested in possibly arranging a phone interview where I might ask her about it and other things, but I was met with the following curt response: "Suella has received your message; however, she has no comments for you." Lovely.

Work cited and/or consulted:
Yellow Tulip Press, Curious Chapbooks & Hysterical Histories Since 1992, *Ask Cousin Suella*, online website

Did Lizzie Borden Axe For It?

III. The Lizzie Shrines

(1) 92 Second Street (Borden house)--Then & Now

Is The House Haunted?
Ghosts At The B&B

An Examination of the Claims That
The Lizzie Borden Bed & Breakfast
Has Ghosts and Paranormal Activity

William H. Moody was a prosecution lawyer in the trial case against Lizzie Borden. His house in Haverhill, Massachussettes is rumored to be haunted. In early 1995 when a family moved in, doors mysteriously opened, and from certain rooms came eerie noises. There's a door that the family never had opened and their dog used to sit and bark at it. They moved out the following month in fright. But few people know about or are interested in that. There's another house that is much more on people's minds.

In August 4, 1995, on the 103rd anniversary of the infamous murders, the Borden house on Second Street ceased to be a private home and, after being transformed by renovations, became the Lizzie Borden B&B. It has offered public tours and office space for the International Lizzie Borden Society. Consisting of 8 rooms

106

and one bathroom, the house attracted and continues to attract people from all over America, Canada, Europe and the rest of the world. Since the murders in 1892, the house spent most of its history as a private residence. Now the public can see the murder scene and even spend the night in the actual house itself where the murders happened. There's the attic room, the bedrooms of Lizzie and Emma, the master bedroom of Andrew and Abby, and most popular of all, not surprisingly, the guest-room where Abby was killed. The late Ron Evans and his business partner, Martha McGinn, opened the bed-and-breakfast with Borden-era antiques and artifacts, Ouija boards, a library of books related to the case, a video collection of the movies it inspired, and occasional murder mystery dinners. Bill Pavao Jr. and Leonard Rebello with their meticulous research are credited with bringing the house back close to the way it looked when the Bordens lived there.

The B&B had been in the McGinn family as a private residence since 1940 and was sold in 2005 to Donald Woods and Lee-ann Wilber. Mr. Woods owns 75% of the property and Miss Wilber owns 25%, but this is not general knowledge; Lee-ann Wilber also runs the place. They have been mentioned in articles as boyfriend and girlfriend and they are "significant others", although they don't live together in the B&B of course, and each has his or her own house.

As soon as it first opened, some guests who spent the night started reporting strange thumping noises, like the body of Abby Borden falling to the floor, or seeing eerie apparitions glowing in the basement. Others swore they heard a woman gently sobbing during the night, saw shoes moving for no apparent reason, impressions appear on newly made beds, a mysterious fog or smoke in the sitting-room, and so on. "Guests are allowed to view the murder scene and can sleep in Lizzie and her sister Emma's bedroom, Abby & Andrew's bedroom or the guest room where Abby was killed. Martha McGinn, former owner and operator, had lived in the house since her teens. Her grandparents had lived in the house for decades. She calls the house 'active' instead of haunted, and believes that the spirits of the murder victims may inhabit the house. Cold spots are felt in many of the rooms. People who work in the house say they have heard many strange sounds, including voices, and unexplained footsteps. Some have seen indentations--like that of a body lying down--appear and disappear on the beds. Objects are mysteriously moved out of place, lights go on and off, and doors and cabinets have opened on their own. Guests have reported seeing an 'older Victorian woman' dusting and making the beds in the guest room as Abby was doing at the time of her death. They have reported being awakened in the night to see this same woman pulling the covers of the bed over them as though she is tucking them in. A couple from Connecticut took a photograph in the sitting room that didn't turn out properly. The photo was almost entirely black except for the apparition of an elderly man who looked very much like Andrew Borden" (*Unexplained Lizzie Borden House*). For the truly adventurous, a stay in the guest-room where Abby was killed should provide a restless night or two. Most of the activity seems to take place in that room. They even have the crime scene photos hanging on the wall in this room. A month after the renovations were complete, a housekeeper claimed she saw an imprint of a body on the bed in there. She ran out of the house and has never returned. There have, also, been reports of disembodied voices, a slamming screen door (there are no screen doors presently in the house), and sounds of furniture being moved around upstairs when no one is upstairs. Psychic activity has also been reported in the attic. According to Martha McGinn, there are doors that open or close by themselves, and "It wasn't just creaks we heard, it was genuine walking," she said. "And there were doors that opened and closed, lights that went on and off." She claims that there are footsteps, mostly at night, always sounding like they are on the floor above the ceiling. During the renovations, friends of Martha were working in

Did Lizzie Borden Axe For It?

the kitchen. They heard furniture being moved around upstairs and thought maybe one of the other helpers had come in. They looked through the house, but no one else was there. And yet, all kinds of strange things about the house had been recorded even long before it opened up as a bed and breakfast. In 1893, a man named Joseph Hurd who lived in the attic became ill up there and apparently died of starvation (*Lizzie Borden: Past & Present*, pp. 30-31). Today the attic where he died is believed to be one of the most haunted parts of the house. The B&B feeds on people's deliciously morbid curiosities and interest in ghosts and the supernatural. One psychic named Jane Doherty even believes that she has Lizzie's voice on tape!

Newly discovered photo of William Moody, a prosecutor in the Lizzie Borden trial, whose house is believed to be haunted-- private collection

Did Lizzie Borden Axe For It?

Lee-ann Wilber, co-owner and manager of the Lizzie Borden Bed & Breakfast. Andrew Borden was murdered while resting on the sitting-room sofa--courtesy Lee-ann Wilber

Did Lizzie Borden Axe For It?

Lee-ann Wilber in the B&B gift-shop--courtesy Ann Abalo

Did Lizzie Borden Axe For It?

Borden house (today)--courtesy Lee-ann Wilber

However, not everyone familiar or connected with the B&B believes in the ghosts (Len Rebello and Bill Pavao have never experienced anything out of the ordinary), but its ghostly reputation helps sell rooms and tours. So, the next time you need a well-deserved vacation, consider staying at the Lizzie Borden Bed and Breakfast in Fall River, Massachusetts. It's an absolute must for Lizzie crime buffs and even for the morbidly curious who know little or nothing about Lizzie. The guest bedroom where Abby was killed costs $250 a night and the other rooms go from $150-$250, depending on the room and the time of year. But it's absolutely worth it for the Lizzie Borden experience. Tours run from 11 a.m. to

Did Lizzie Borden Axe For It?

3:00 p.m. Under its new ownership, the B&B is now open all year round, although closed on major holidays. Adult admission is $10.00; $8.00 for seniors; children 7-12, $5.00. Children under 7 are free. The tour is also free for guests spending the night. Phototaking is allowed in the house. For more information or reservations, call (508) 675-7333. Also check out the website at **lizzie-borden.com**

Works cited and/or consulted:
Jon Marcus, *Famed Lizzie Borden House May Become Inn*
Unexplained Lizzie Borden House, author unknown
Leonard Rebello, *Lizzie Borden: Past & Present*

Did Lizzie Borden Axe For It?

The Borden house (today), which is also a popular bed and breakfast--courtesy Lee-ann Wilber

Did Lizzie Borden Axe For It?

(2) Maplecroft--Then & Now

In July 1893, a few weeks after the trial was over, Lizzie and Emma purchased and moved into a thirteen-room, gray, half-stone Victorian house on French Street, situated on "The Hill", the most fashionable, prestigious residential area in Fall River. Lizzie was so pleased with the house that she actually gave it a name--"Maplecroft"--and had the name chiseled into the top stone step leading up to the front door, which was an extravagance that went against high society norms of etiquette and was a sign to the elite of "The Hill" that Lizzie was trying to be better than she was. The carving makes the home easier to spot from the street today. However, the fact of the matter is that Lizzie and Emma could have easily afforded one of the much more grand and ostentatious mansions in the Highlands district, but opted for the cheaper and more understated Maplecroft on French Street, probably to avoid criticism. It cost them, at most, 13 thousand dollars--no small sum in those days, but no fortune either, especially given the hundreds of thousands of dollars that Lizzie and Emma inherited. It was a good, over-sized, reasonably impressive upper-middle-class home, but nothing more.

Some time after moving into her new home, Lizzie was referring to herself as "Lizbeth" or "Lizbeth of Maplecroft." The house had 13 rooms. "She now had four bathrooms instead of none and all the animals she wanted instead of the pigeons her father decapitated" (Ruth Whitman). Here she would live out the rest of

115

Did Lizzie Borden Axe For It?

her days in comfortable seclusion, looked after by her maids and servants, kept company by her pet Boston bull terriers, Donald Stuart, Royal Nelson and Laddie Miller. She had an extensive library to occupy her time as she had always been an avid reader. Her many books, and other possessions, "were distributed according to her wishes among her family, staff and remaining friends following her death. She was remembered by some who knew her in later life as a lady of great kindness and generosity, with a fondness for children and animals."

But rumors about her continued to spread. One involved a frightened deliveryman who allegedly brought a wooded crate to Maplecroft; he ran off in terror when Lizzie offered to get an axe for him! "As she became the eccentric who was preoccupied with [feeding] birds and squirrels and the welfare of animals in general, she became the seldom-seen legend who refused to leave Fall River, except for occasional and mysterious trips to Boston, New York, and Washington, D.C., glimpsed riding in her chauffeured limousine."

The late Russell Lake was just a child when Lizzie lived in Maplecroft, but he remembered Lizzie as "the nicest little old lady I ever knew."

An obscure Scottish poem by Allan Cunningham is carved into the fireplace mantel at Maplecroft:

The green leaf of loyalty's beginning to fall.
The bonnie White Rose it is withering an' all.
But I'll water it with the blood of usurping tyranny,
And green it will grow in my ain countree.

One could interpret this poem in several ways. Here's one possible take on it--first line: Andrew has betrayed Lizzie by taking sides with Abby; second line: their relationship has withered; line three:

116

Did Lizzie Borden Axe For It?

but I'll spill your blood because of this betrayal, says Lizzie; and, line four: in the afterlife you, father, will be loyal to me again! Given Lizzie's supposedly odd mentality, this interpretation makes a whole lot of sense when applied to her.

For the 34 years that Lizzie lived in her Maplecroft home before her death, she never consented to sit down for any interview, although there were several requests from reporters and journalists. Not once did she publicly speak out about the case.

Today, Maplecroft is a white-painted, big, sprawling Queen Anne style house which looks somewhat to be in a state of being rundown. It's a private residence, which it has always been since Lizzie's death, and is (or was) also at times open as a museum and bed-and-breakfast inn, with an adjacent carriage house. The building bears many touches just as Lizzie left them and still displays the originality and character of the 1890s. Unlike the neighborhood of 92 Second Street, French Street retains its turn-of-the-century architecture, although many houses have been split into apartments or small businesses. Maplecroft is owned by an insurance adjuster named Robert Dube. The Providence Journal article *Town Offers Insight into Axe Suspect* points out that he gave "tours that give an intimate flavor of Lizzie's personality, with little reference to the murders themselves." Hours: 11 a.m. to 3 p.m. daily, but always best to call ahead; call 508-673-8088. But be prepared to have your request for tours turned down or to get the answering machine. Also, leaving a message doesn't necessarily mean you'll be called back. But if you do manage to get the Dube family at a good time and decide to make a reservation to spend the night, the gourmet homemade breakfast is good and it's a thrill to sleep in a room in which Lizzie herself slept. Bear in mind however that the house is officially no longer a B&B and special arrangements would need to

Did Lizzie Borden Axe For It?

be agreed upon.

In fact, the Maplecroft house was on sale. The Borden house, too, has been sold. A big part of the reason why the Lizzie shrines have been on the market recently is that they didn't make their owners enough money as B&B's. We really, really could use a renaissance of interest in the case, and a good (or great) new Lizzie movie would do that like nothing else. That is *exactly* what happened with L.M. Montgomery's *Anne of Green Gables* when the hit film came out in 1985. It brought Anne back *big*. I'm talking millions of new devotees, not just a few thousand as is the case with Lizzie these days. The Borden case has all the ingredients of a big hit, it just needs a well-done new Hollywood movie to catapult it back into the American psyche in a big way.

Mr. Dube, as owner of Maplecroft, went to the Fall River zoning board and tried to get another building put on the property. He got much bad press over it. He ended up taking it off the market, forgetting about putting the building up, and the last I heard he nailed a board over the "Maplecroft" carving on the front step in disgust! What happened to Dube is deplorable. I very firmly disagree with what Dube wanted to do, but I'm even more dismayed by all these people who think it's their right to tell him what he must do with *his own* property. I know many of us consider Maplecroft sacred and a historical landmark, but he is the guy who with his own hard-earned money bought and owns it, he should be able in a democratic society to do or not to do whatever he pleases with it. What happened to him is an example of the ever-encroaching cloud of mind-fascism and organized coercion we see in our times and he caved in to it. If he hadn't backed down, his life I'm sure would have been made miserable. Maplecroft is not designated a historical heritage site as far as I know, and it's not like he was planning to tear the place down anyway. Again, I oppose the building he wanted to put up, but I oppose even more strongly people who act like Maplecroft belongs to *them* and that Dube better do as *they* say.

Did Lizzie Borden Axe For It?

Recent photo of Maplecroft; it has since been re-painted-- courtesy Steven Cambra

Did Lizzie Borden Axe For It?

Rear of Maplecroft (today)--courtesy Faye Musselman

Did Lizzie Borden Axe For It?

Works cited and/or consulted:
Russell Aiuto, *Lizzie Borden*
Ruth Whitman, *Who Took the Axe and Gave the Whacks?*
The Lizzie Borden Myth in American Popular Culture, author unknown
The Fall River Historical Society: *Profiles of Textual References, Miss Lizzie Andrew Borden*
Anne Stuart, *A Century Later Crime Buffs Still Seek Clues In Lizzie Borden Case*
Stephen R. Jendrysik, *Suspicion Still Clouds Lizzie Borden Case*
The Providence Journal, October 29, 2000

(3) The Fall River Historical Society--Then & Now

Founded in 1921, the Fall River Historical Society's mission is to preserve and protect all manner of artifacts relating to the rich and varied history of the city of Fall River, Massachusetts. The Historical Society is housed in a granite mansion, built in 1843 in the same Greek Revival style as the Borden house, although much more grand.

In 1870, the building was dismantled and moved three-quarters of a mile north to its present location on Rock Street. Enlarged and redesigned in the then-fashionable French Second Empire style, the structure was owned by a very wealthy family and became the scene of a number of glittering social affairs. Of particular note was a wedding reception to which 500 privileged guests were invited, chosen from the over 2000 invited to the ceremony. In order to accommodate the guests, a 20-foot by 50-foot pavilion was erected off the circular dining room, only to be dismantled the following day. Covered extensively by the press, it was noted that "the array of beautiful dresses was probably never equaled in this city" and that "the display of diamonds was extensive."

The house was later sold to one of Fall River's most prominent textile magnates and remained in his family for the next fifty-seven years. Then in 1935 the house was donated to the Fall River Historical Society. It's one of the few surviving examples in Fall River, Massachusetts, of mansions built by the affluent mill

Did Lizzie Borden Axe For It?

owners during the period of the city's greatest prosperity.

In addition, the Historical Society also maintains another house constructed in 1870 and situated on property adjacent to the museum building. This structure is called the Florence Cook Brigham Annex in honor of the Society's beloved late curator. She was succeeded by the charming and very capable Michael Martins.

The Fall River Historical Society maintains the world's largest collection of artifacts relating to the life and trial of Miss Lizzie A. Borden, defendant in one of the most famous murder cases in American history. Miss Borden, the thirty-two-year-old spinster daughter of prominent Fall River businessman Andrew Borden, was accused of the vicious murders of both her father and his second wife, Abby. In August of 1892, the two were found brutally slain in their Fall River home, their skulls smashed and shattered by what was later determined to be a hatchet-like weapon. The sensational trial which followed made headlines worldwide; it is considered to be the crime of that century. Although Miss Borden was eventually acquitted of both murders, even today the very mention of Lizzie's name can provoke a heated, passionate debate . . . did she or didn't she?

The saga of Lizzie Borden has never ended. A number of plays, musicals and even an opera have been penned about her. The A&E Television Network produced an hour-long video biography (available on VHS) and both the Discovery and History Channels have produced programs about her life. From the Broadway musical New Faces of 1952 came the song "You Can't Chop Your Papa up in Massachusetts" and, of course, who doesn't remember the infamous rhyme "Lizzie Borden took an axe . . . "

It's all here for you to see: the handleless hatchet, her prison lunch pail, the police photographs taken at the scene of the crime, the billy club the arresting officer carried, the pillow shams from the bedroom that Abby was murdered in, the photographs of Andrew and Abby's crushed skulls introduced as evidence, the braided

Did Lizzie Borden Axe For It?

hairpiece that Abby was wearing when she was so nefariously attacked . . . and enough material in our archive to attract historians, scholars, playwrights, researchers and filmmakers from the far corners of the globe. The FRHS is located at 451 Rock Street, Fall River; open Mon. to Fri. 9 a.m. to 4:30 p.m., Sat. to Sun. 1 p.m. to 5 p.m.; phone (508) 679-1071. The website address is: **lizzieborden.org**

For anyone interested in the Borden case, the collection at the Fall River Historical Society is a must-see. After all, when it comes to the evidence and actual courtroom exhibits, we have it all. Examine the evidence and decide for yourself: "Guilty" or "Not Guilty."

--The Fall River Historical Society; Used with Permission

The Fall River Historical Society (today)--from the Keeley Library, B. M. C. Durfee High School, courtesy Ron Bettencourt

Did Lizzie Borden Axe For It?

(4) Central Congregational Church--Then & Now

Rock Street leads you up a hill, and the first thing you see walking up is the Central Congregational Church on the left, between Bank and Franklin Streets. It was built in 1875 and to this day is thought of by many as the most beautiful church edifice in Fall River. The church is made out of fine red brick and sandstone, designed in the early English Gothic style, with its towering spire. There you'd have found the old Borden family pew. The Borden pew was number 22, and although it has long since been removed, it was located near "the back of the church, just to the right of the far left side aisle."

Prior to 1885, the Borden family had been members of the First Congregational Church, but Lizzie started attending church at the Central Congregational Church at 282 Rock St and was an active member from about the age of 25 onwards. "A few years before the murder she joined the Central Congregational church and was oft-times an active member of that society" (*The Fall River Tragedy*, p. 22). It was the "in" church, where the Hill's elite worshipped. She was the only regular church-goer in the family. Lizzie became very active in church charity activities, like the Fruit and Flower Mission, and taught at the mission chapel. It was reported that "The Bible class, the Sunday school and the prayer meeting were about the most exciting of her pleasures."

Seabury Bowen, the family physician who lived across the street from the Bordens, once took Lizzie to church with him in his carriage when her parents were vacationing away at Swansea and she was alone in the house. They were seen arriving and sitting together at church and this sparked rumors of an affair.

Years later, when she was acquitted at trial of the crime of familicide, "[Lizzie] determinedly dressed for services and took her place in the family pew at Central Congregational Church. Every seat around hers was empty." Needless to say, she soon stopped attending. The way some people there started to keep their distance and others troubled her with nagging unanswered questions about the murders and her firmly alleged innocence, it must have been all too unpleasant for her. Jonathan Thayer Lincoln, later to become father of well-known Lizzie Borden author Victoria Lincoln, wrote in a letter to his lady-love Mattie Davol: "the town was all astir Sunday because Lizzie Borden went to church. I don't see why it should bother people so, for if she is guilty, is not church the best place for her?"

Vida L. Turner was the soloist from Central Congregational Church, and she was asked to sing "My Ain Countree", the old Scottish hymn, at the Maplecroft house after Lizzie died. According to former Fall River Historical Society curator, the late Florence C. Brigham (1899-2000), Mrs. Turner came to the house and rang the bell. A gentleman answered and told her to follow him; he told her to stand right by the fireplace. So, in the words of Vida Turner, "I stood there and sang that song to an empty room. I never saw a soul but that one man."

The Central Congregational Church is today the International Culinary Institute and the ideal spot for Borden buffs to stop for a bite to eat. As the *Providence Journal* points out, "The red-and-yellow brick spire of the former Central Congregational Church remains an impressive fixture on the city's skyline. Not a lot to see at the International Culinary Institute regarding the Bordens, but what could be a more appropriate place for a meal while on the

Did Lizzie Borden Axe For It?

Lizzie Borden tour?"

George Karousos, a master chef who all his life dreamed about owning and running such an establishment, opened the school in 1997. He invested very heavily in the equipment and construction costs, but said that the primary aim was not to make a profit. "The idea is not to make money because we believe so much in education," said Mr. Karousos, who also runs the five-star Sea Fare Inn in Portsmouth, R.I., and the Sea Fare's American Cafe in Newport, R. I. "We believe the next generation of chefs has to be educated. Not only do you have to be a good chef, you have to be a good businessman. Students must not only focus on the kitchen, but the relationships in the restaurant business between customers and restaurants." His aim is to pass his vision and passion for good cooking on to a new generation of chefs, to teach them the secrets of the trade. He believes in giving them a first-rate culinary education by way of hands-on training. "The students learn as much from the professors as they do from the customers of Abby Grill. It is a type of immersion into the work place that he [Mr. Karousos] says is the key ingredient for a successful crop of chefs. "You have to serve the food yourself and see the reaction of the customers," he said. "You have to listen to the complaints and very politely, you have to correct it."

The institute offers lunch meals from Monday to Friday and dinner from Thursday to Saturday. The lunches are cheap and good, prepared by the students. The menus change from week to week and are a reflection of what the students learn. The current address is 100 Rock St., and the entrance is left of the church. No longer a church, it is now known as the Abbey Grille, located in the former parish house. The main eating room is "the grill". It's an impressive dining room "dominated by a stained-glass window, a crystal chandelier and the open-air kitchen/laboratory supervised by the school's instructors."

No need to travel to France or Italy to have fine European

Did Lizzie Borden Axe For It?

dining, you can find it right there at Lizzie's church in Fall River!

Works cited and/or consulted:
Lizzie Borden's Church - Central Congregational Church, Fall River, MA, author unknown
The Boston Daily Globe, June 21, 1893
The Providence Journal, October 29, 2000
The Hartford Courant, May 11, 2001
The New York Times, July 26, 1992
The Standard-Times, August 9, 1997
Edwin H. Porter, *The Fall River Tragedy*
The Witness Statements For the Lizzie Borden Murder Case
Excerpt from a letter by (Jonathan) Thayer Lincoln

Did Lizzie Borden Axe For It?

Central Congregational Church (today) where Lizzie worshipped. She stopped attending services some time after her acquittal, reportedly because she was made to feel unwelcome-- private collection

Did Lizzie Borden Axe For It?

(5) Swansea--Then & Now

Swansea and the surrounding areas are quite interesting with their historical colonial sites, nice beaches, good restaurants, working farms, wineries, brewery, galleries and shops. In Lizzie's day (as well as our own), it boasted some of the best sailing, hiking, biking, and fresh and saltwater fishing.

In 1871 when Lizzie was still a small girl, Andrew Borden and his business partner William Almy together bought the two lots of land that make up the Swansea property for three thousand dollars. Lot #1 was described as "Situated on easterly side of highway leading from Swansea Village through Gardners Neck, so called." Lot #2 was "Situated on westerly side of highway and extending west to the salt water, thence northerly to land of said railroad. Containing in the whole 10 acres and 136 rods more or less . . ." When Almy died in 1885, Andrew bought out the rest of the property.

With the death of her father in 1892, Lizzie's beloved summer home in Swansea was one of the estates that she and Emma inherited. It's situated just across the Taunton River to the west of Swansea, on one of the two farms. It was here that Lizzie and her sister "frolicked in their youth", as true-crime author Walter Hixson put it. She also loved to fish at Swansea in those earlier years. In adulthood, Lizzie still loved to come there to relax, especially in the warm months of the year. She would run her dogs around the field and take country walks along the lanes. This is also the place where

Did Lizzie Borden Axe For It?

Lizzie was rumored to have had secret trysts with "Mr. Gardner."

Today it's a private residence situated at 1205 Gardner's Neck Road, a short drive from Fall River. It sits close to the road and nowadays is surrounded by newer houses on each side and across the street. Nevertheless, it's easily recognizable, though the hedges that existed in front of the house in Lizzie's day have been removed. This old farmhouse is only a few miles west across Mount Hope Bay and is accessible from Fall River's downtown area. Today it's part of what appears to be largely a suburban residential development neighborhood. In the late 19th century it was mostly open fields (mowings and pasture) and woodlots with land sloping down to the bay. The Swansea house is not on the water but is quite near to it. With open fields and only a handful of neighboring houses and farms, it must have afforded a picturesque, beautiful view of the bay to the east and south across the water towards neighboring areas of Rhode Island. Furthermore, it's easy to see why such a tranquil place satisfied Lizzie's taste for peaceful seclusion. The area where the house is located is an easy walk from the shoreline of Mount Hope Bay. This is where Lizzie fished in the bay.

The Swansea house was sold and bought several times from the time that Lizzie inherited to now, and there are very few traces of her left there. But I was recently rather amused to see that a meat-cleaver from the Swansea farmhouse (and once owned by Lizzie) was put up for sale at an auction.

Works cited and/or consulted:
Walter L. Hixson, *Gendered Justice: Lizzie Borden and Victorian America*

Did Lizzie Borden Axe For It?

Fall River Area Chamber of commerce and industry (Area Attractions), author unknown
The 1871 Land Transaction Deed for the Swansea Property

The summer home at Swansea (today), where Lizzie is supposed to have met her alleged lover Orrin Gardner--courtesy Faye Musselman

(6) Oak Grove Cemetery

Josiah Brown was the local mill architect who designed Oak Grove Cemetery, located at the head of Prospect Street in Fall River. He modelled it after Mt. Auburn Cemetery in Cambridge, Mass. At the time, the city bought the land from a man named Nathan Durfee for the minor sum of two hundred dollars an acre. It originally encompassed some 47 acres. Today located at 765 Prospect St., Oak Grove Cemetery has a beautiful entrance, and on the left-hand side as you walk in you'll see the monument works of Alexander Lawson. Here monuments, headstones, curbing, and all kinds of cemetery work in marble and granite were executed in excellent taste and style. There are also oak leaves and ivy leaves engraved into various headstones, symbolizing strength, faith and devotion. Of the many statues and monuments, there is one "devoted to Richard Borden, one of the founders of the Fall River Line. The statue portrays him holding a boat anchor that many believed was Lizzie Borden holding the ax possibly used in the notorious murder." Today, this graveyard is very old and many of the graves are in disrepair.

The Borden name is the most prevalent in the cemetery, although not all are related to Lizzie. Lizzie is the most famous, the most popular (and the most visited) resident of Oak Grove Cemetery. It is the last resting place of one of the (and perhaps *the*) most famous and infamous alleged murderesses who ever lived. Obviously many tourists and visitors to Fall River asked about

Did Lizzie Borden Axe For It?

Lizzie, because when you enter the cemetery, you'll see arrows painted on the road leading from the cemetery gate right to her family plot at Lat: 41`42'24"N, Lon: 071`08'15"W.

According to FRHS curator Michael Martins and his archivists, banquets at Lizzie's grave are quite common. When people come to him expressing their interest in or admiration for Lizzie, Martins and his staff tell them where she's buried. These devotees then often go over to Oak Grove to pay their homage with wine or flowers. The grave is most decorated with flowers on significant days, like Lizzie's birthday, the day of the murders, the day of her acquittal, and the day of her death. People used to make requests and send checks from all over the country asking that flowers be put on the grave. But, says Martins, "We always return the money. We're not in the flower business." When he was talking about Lizzie's admirers, Jules Ryckebusch once said, "Some always want to recognize a special date in regard to Lizzie." According to him, when Lizzie died, the Fall River animal shelter to which she had given a considerable bequest, for years put flowers on her grave in gratitude and appreciation.

Lizzie died of heart failure on June 2, 1927. Emma didn't go to the funeral; on the day of Lizzie's death, Emma fell down a flight of stairs and broke her hip. Some people allege that Emma attempted suicide by throwing herself down the stairs in her wheelchair on purpose when she learned of Lizzie's death. Is this suicide rumor true? At any rate, Emma died just 9 days after Lizzie. Both were buried on the Borden family plot. "Andrew Borden lies between Sarah and Abbey, his wives, while Lizzie and Emma are at his feet. A grant made to the city of Fall River in Lizzie's will pays for the perpetual upkeep of the plot. Lizzie's tomb is just a few steps away from the final resting place of her alleged victims. At the time of her death, Lizzie had not spoken to her sister in twenty-two years." Since Lizzie and Emma had no children, there are only a few distant relatives around these days, and no direct descendants.

Did Lizzie Borden Axe For It?

As with the Borden house on Second Street, ghost-hunters claim that Oak Grove Cemetery is haunted. "Witnesses report seeing lights in the cemetery and some have even heard screaming from the Borden family plot."

Works cited and/or consulted:
The Herald News, September 30, 2002
The Visitor's Guide to Bristol County, author unknown
Carole D. Bos, LawBuzz--*Famous Trials, Lizzie Borden*
Shadowlands Haunted Places in Massachusetts, author unknown

NOTE: There are three other Lizzie "shrines" worth mentioning but they no longer exist. There is Lizzie's grandfather's house where she was born at 12 Ferry Street, which my notes tell me was turned into a refuse-filled vacant lot. And there is also Taunton jail, which was torn down. Also worth mentioning is her high school which too was torn down and the B. M. C. Durfee High School was built in its place.

Did Lizzie Borden Axe For It?

Entrance to Oak Grove Cemetery (today)--courtesy Little Theater of Fall River

Did Lizzie Borden Axe For It?

*Overhead view of Oak Grove Cemetery (today) where the
Bordens are all buried--courtesy Sheri White*

Did Lizzie Borden Axe For It?

Lizzie's high school no longer stands, but this is the building (today) where she went to elementary school. It was called the Morgan Street Grammar School, and today it's the N. B. Borden School--courtesy the Fall River Historical Society Collection

IV. Miscellaneous

1. Articles

I've written numerous separate original essays or articles on the Lizzie case and here is a sample of those which I feel are most suitable for inclusion in book form rather than another medium. Some of them vary dramatically in theme and subject-matter, although all are related in one way or another to Lizzie and Bordenia.

What Lizzie's Defense Team Really Thought of Her

There's nothing more fascinating to me than trying to find out what a defense lawyer actually privately thinks of his client when we're dealing with someone accused of murder. Is the lawyer fond of his client? Does he believe he can "get him off"? Does he believe him innocent or guilty? And if he believes his client guilty, can he in

Did Lizzie Borden Axe For It?

good conscience defend him to the best of his ability? Edward Radin in his book on the case quotes the advice a judge once gave a young lawyer: "If the attorney believes his client innocent, put him on the witness stand without hesitation, if however, he believes him guilty, never put him on the witness stand." This advice to me seems too simplistic. Even if it's good advice for most cases, it cannot be good advice for all cases.

First of all, what did Lizzie think of her own lawyers? Edmund L. Pearson writes in his *Trial of Lizzie Borden*, page 84, that "She never liked Mr. Jennings, but adored the memory of Governor Robinson."

There was a rumor at the time that Lizzie's lawyer, George Dexter Robinson, had a private meeting with Lizzie in Taunton jail and needed Lizzie to assure him that she was innocent for him to agree to represent her as attorney (*Lizzie Borden Past & Present*, p. 198). This may or may not be true. What is certain is that George D. Robinson was fond of Lizzie and defended her very effectively at trial. Prosecutor Knowlton's slightly confused and half-heartedly pursued factual reasonings were no match for Robinson's highly clever emotional arguments.

It's interesting to contemplate how even part of Lizzie's defense team seems to have believed she was guilty--Andrew Jennings and Melvin Adams. After the trial, Jennings refused to have anything to do with Lizzie and refused to have her name mentioned or to speak about how she may have slaughtered his good friend Andy (*Goodbye Lizzie Borden*, p. 63; *Lizzie Borden, Past and Present*, p. 304). Adams, who seems to have been a man without qualms about making unethical choices and connections (see *The Witness Statements*, p. 23), agreed to represent Lizzie against his wife's wishes. In fact, Adams' wife Mary Colony was peeved off at him for defending "this woman, when *you know* she is guilty" (Ibid.).

But Robinson remained a close and loyal friend and ally to

Did Lizzie Borden Axe For It?

Lizzie until his death in 1896 just a few years after the trial. Arthur S. Phillips, a law student and assistant to Jennings who had helped accumulate evidence for the defense team, remained firmly convinced of her innocence all his life. He wrote *The Borden Murder Mystery*. Phillips lived to a fairly ripe old age, dying in 1941.

Clearly there was a deep-seated conflict of opinion about the woman within the defense team, but it was almost certainly kept quiet and under wraps; Lizzie was paying Robinson $25, 000 for his legal representation, and in those days that was the equivalent of almost $500, 000 in today's money--that may be enough to silence any conscience.

Works cited and/or consulted:
Edmund Lester Pearson, *Trial of Lizzie Borden*
Edward D. Radin, *Lizzie Borden, The Untold Story*
Arthur S. Phillips, *The Borden Murder Mystery: In Defense of Lizzie Borden*
Leonard Rebello, *Lizzie Borden Past & Present*
The Witness Statements For the Lizzie Borden Murder Case
Robert Sullivan, *Goodbye Lizzie Borden*

NOTE: Jennings, in his *opening statement for the defense* at the trial, says this: "I want to make a personal allusion before referring directly to the case. One of the victims of the murder charged in this indictment was for many years my client and my personal friend. I had known him since my boyhood. I had known his oldest daughter for the same length of time, and I want to say right here and now, if I manifest more feeling than perhaps you think necessary in making an opening statement for the defence in this case, you will ascribe it to that cause. The counsel, Mr. Foreman and gentlemen, does not cease to be a man when he becomes a lawyer."

Did Lizzie Borden Axe For It?

A Conspiracy of Melvin Adams, Edwin HcHenry and Henry Trickey

Contained in the *Witness Statements*, pp. 22-26 is a lengthy passage where Police Captain Philip Harrington went to Detective Edwin P. McHenry's house in Providence on the evening of September 29, 1892 and wound up eavesdropping on a private conversation in the parlor between McHenry and Henry G. Trickey, the esteemed young journalist for the *Boston Daily Globe*. Incidentally, Melvin Adams was later to be tricked for money (500$) by McHenry with what was fabricated prosecution evidence, unbeknownst to Trickey.

Interestingly, Harrington concealed himself and got close enough to hear almost every single word. He wrote the whole conversation down in shorthand. It appears that Trickey was getting information from certain Fall River police officers about what evidence the prosecution had against Lizzie, and selling it to Melvin Ohio Adams, counsel for Miss Borden. The inference is that Andrew Jennings and Lizzie, herself, were in on it (clearly the money paid by Adams to Trickey would have come from Lizzie). Apparently Jennings had reservations about these shady dealings but caved in. At one point, Trickey asked Adams if he thought Lizzie was guilty. Adams declined to answer, but showed him a letter from his wife wherein she got angry with her husband for joining Lizzie's defense team.

This is all very interesting stuff, and I wonder why more hasn't been made of it. If it's true, it seems highly unethical (and probably illegal) for Adams to have dealt this way--buying alleged evidence against Lizzie from HcHenry through Trickey, agreeing to pay them $500 each; and if Trickey is telling the truth, he also bought classified evidence material for his articles from Fall River police officers and their friends, which includes Officer Medley; it appears even Mayor Coughlin was bought by Trickey for inside evidence which only the police and prosecutor's office were privy to! As for Lizzie, she apparently paid $1,000 to get the scoop on the prosecution's evidence, according to Trickey. If Harrington's note-taking recording of the conversation is legit, and there's no evidence to suggest we should disbelieve it, then that's exactly what was happening! This by itself certainly doesn't prove that Lizzie committed the murders, but it does by no means paint her and her lawyers in a good light. Likewise, this information makes prominent members of the Fall River Police look like corrupt bribe-takers. This is probably why Harrington didn't do more with this gold mine against Lizzie. It would have caused a scandalous outcry again some of his fellow police buddies as well.

Here are the most relevant excerpts; pay particular attention to the passages I have italicized:
(Trickey) "Begorry, I waited up there until I got tired. ***Well, Mr. I fixed the deal with Adams; there is $1000 to be had for the prosecution's case*** . . . *Mel. Adams has the $1000 ready to pay over the minute the evidence of the prosecution was obtained by him. I will come down tomorrow night, and get the whole business [prosecution evidence], take it to Adams, get the money, and turn it over to you. The first proposition made to me, as you know, was $500. That came from Adams; but the $1000 was later agreed to by Jennings, Adam having sent for him, and talked the matter over. He, Jennings, then went and saw Lizzie, and she assented to it, and Jennings wrote Adams it was all right.* ***Jennings then called on Adams, and told him he had seen***

Did Lizzie Borden Axe For It?

Lizzie, and she agreed to: the proposition, so the money will be paid. There will be $500 for you, and $500 for me."

(McHenry) *"You know, Trickey, they [Lizzie's defense team] are not looking for the murderer."*

(Trickey) *"Why, of course not, all they want is the evidence of the government. Now let me tell you something, Mr. I asked Mel. Adams if he thought Lizzie was not guilty. He said, "I am counsel for her, and cannot speak; but here is something I will show you." He handed me a letter which was from his wife, and it read something like this; "I am ashamed to think that my husband has interested himself in the defence of this woman, when you know she is guilty. You had no business to have anything to do with her case."*

(McHenry) "Now Trickey, what do you think of Jennings? Did you see him to talk about this matter?"

(Trickey) "No, I am doing business with Adams. He, Adams, said Jennings was a provincial fellow, and doesn't know anything. When he was spoken to about this deal, at first he would not do it. I could do nothing with him, he is too much of a Puritan. I suppose you know Adams got Hanscom [a detective hired by Lizzie/Emma] into this case. They are great friends. It was Adams who defended Hanscom when in trouble with the Boston Police."

(Trickey) "Adams stands well with the Pinkertons. *He [Adams] is a pretty shrewd fellow, and stands well in with the crooks. When he was Asst. District Attorney, he would go to them, and assure them he had nothing against them, and then say, "did you do this? I won't be hard on you." You know what this meant, so as to get their business when he got out of office. As I said before, he defended Hanscom at his hearing before the Police Commission. They are both good friends, and always work together."*

(McHenry) "Trickey, you must have a step on Seaver [a detective working with the Fall River police], getting information in this case while you were in Fall River."

Did Lizzie Borden Axe For It?

(Trickey) "No, Mr. Seaver only gave me the ground work every day to go do. For instance, he would say, today the ax is the principal subject. The next day, the tip would be the bottle of [prussic] acid, and so on. It is true he gave me such tips every day I saw him, but he did not give me everything; that is, he would not give me the whole subject. He would merely hint at the subject and then I would go to work. *I get the most of my information indirectly from Harrington and Doherty. The prussic acid story, I got indirectly from them through a friend of theirs to whom I gave $25. The party to whom I gave up the $25 is a policeman on the inside.*"

(McHenry) *"How about Medley?"*

(Trickey) *"Oh, pshaw, he is cheap. I got him anytime for a couple of beers.* He is the cheapest chump of them all.

(McHenry) *"Well, how about the Mayor [Coughlin]?"*

(Trickey) "He was one of my best friends. *I got a great deal [of private information] from him. He is a dandy for staying up nights. I tell you he gave me lots of good news. Now about the deal with Adams; I can't see him tonight, as he lives out of town, I think in Worchester; but I will see him about 8.30 A. M. tomorrow morning.* After nine o'clock nobody can find him; sometimes he goes to Cambridge."

(McHenry) "How about advancing some money now as a retainer?"

(Trickey) "Well, of course I cannot do so now, for I haven't got the stuff; but Adams is thoroughly honest, I know this, for I have worked with him before; and as soon as you have this evidence ready, there will be no delay about the money." [Note: McHenry's "evidence" published by Trickey in the *Boston Globe* turned out to be fabricated, "made up"].

(McHenry) "Now, old man, how will this money be paid, in cash or check? You know a check can be very easily stopped."

(Trickey) "He does not do business that way. I would trust Adams with anything. You may come to Boston with me, or not. Perhaps it would be better not to be seen in Boston together, the Pinkertons might catch on. What time will it be convenient for you to see me tomorrow?

(McHenry) "Make it late in the afternoon, I am not feeling well."

(Trickey) "I will leave Boston about 3. P. M. and arrive here about 6. P. M. Have your notes ready, and arrange them like this; John Jones, No.---street, will testify as follows; . . . Three or four days before we publish this, I will go to Fall River, and spend much time there among these people, and put some time in around Jennings' office, and no one will be able to tell where the story came from. Neither you nor I can afford to lose our reputation for $500. And if you give me straight goods, we can get---(here I lost what was said for a while). Do you think that from what the government has got, Lizzie will be convicted?"

(McHenry) "Why, yes . . . "

(Trickey) *". . . Adams when talking about this case, said, I think I will soon give up this criminal business, and go entirely into the civil. I am getting tired of trying to keep criminals out of jail, and the rope away from their necks.' . . . Give your word that the evidence is valuable, and is only a matter of turning the evidence over to Adams* [It bears repeating that this "evidence" from McHenry was of course a fabrication], *and I know the money will be all right."*

(McHenry) "Now Trickey, I am thinking it is not asking too much of you to give me some money [now]."

(Trickey) "That is just what I want myself, as my creditors are pushing me for a couple of hundred dollars, and the sooner this thing is settled, the better it will be . . . "

Did Lizzie Borden Axe For It?

Work cited and/or consulted:
The Witness Statements for the Lizzie Borden Murder Case

A newly discovered photo of Melvin Adams, a defense attorney for Lizzie Borden who offered Trickey and McHenry 1,000$ for what he and the defense team mistakenly thought would be genuine prosecution evidence--private collection

Did Lizzie Borden Axe For It?

Uncovering Nance O'Neil

I. Nance's Life & Career

Nance O'Neil was born Gertrude Lamson on October 8, 1874 in Oakland, California. For a Victorian woman, she was very tall at 5'8 and was described as stately in appearance, with a beautiful eloquent voice, which was low and appealing in regular conversation, but capable of loud, bold vigor on stage. She was also described as blonde, Amazonian and passionate. Her father was a well-to-do auctioneer in San Francisco, who abhorred the idea that his daughter wanted to become an actress.

Agent-actor McKee Rankin discovered the Oakland-born O'Neil when his own company played San Francisco in 1893; she was 19 years old. She had a letter of introduction from the drama critic of *The Chronicle*. It read "Here is a young friend of mine who wants to go on the stage. Kindly discourage her."

Nance made her acting debut at the Alcazar Theatre in San Francisco in October of the same year. Rankin cast her in a small part as a nun in his production, but only realized her great gifts when he cast her in another play as Captain Tommy, a mining camp prostitute. Then came a season in which she played Shakespeare and Ibsen, in Boston. From then on he nurtured her with an attention that led the press to suggest they were lovers. Under his tutelage she gained her fame in the United States and abroad. When they eventually broke in 1908, he sued her. Most observers, however,

149

Did Lizzie Borden Axe For It?

saw her independence from him as long overdue. The court dismissed his suit. Nance had become an acclaimed tragedienne and a major stage star, playing the likes of Lady Macbeth, Hedda Gabler, and Camille. When she played Boston in 1904, she eventually had the city "Nance O'Neil mad," as a Boston paper put it. Before leaving the city, she played at three of its most prominent theaters. At the height of her popularity, the newspapers were reporting that Nance O'Neil was having an "intimate" relationship with the so-called murderess Lizzie Borden, and there were hints that the friendship was romantic. Nance's career revived somewhat after the low years of 1905-8. When she opened in the production of *The Lily* at the end of 1909, a critic for the *New York Evening News* wrote, "And so, at last, after fifteen years of constant struggle and strife, of bitter disaster and fleeting provincial triumph, a great American actress at last came into her own."

A notorious spendthrift always in financial trouble, O'Neil finally left the New York stage for Hollywood and ended up in more than a few bit parts, especially in movies of the early '30s. She was one of the first of her generation of stage actresses to embrace the financial lure of motion pictures. Signing with producer William Fox, she starred in a 1915 screen version of Leo Tolstoy's *The Kreutzer Sonata*. Although receiving favorable reviews, the veteran star was somewhat upstaged by the colorful Theda Bara, and it was Bara who would become Fox's major dramatic star, not the aging O'Neil. The latter continued to appear in films through 1917-- including playing *Hedda Gabler* again in the lead role, and the Czarina in *The Fall of the Romanoffs*--but moviegoers never truly warmed up to her and she returned to the stage. Her first speaking role on film occurred in 1929 in the ill-fated *His Glorious Night*. O'Neil lent her considerable presence to scores of early talkies, appearing in over 30 British and American films, including as the mother superior in *Call of the Flesh*, and unbilled as Mrs. Von Stael in *Westward Passage*. She played Felice Venable in *Cimmaron*,

Did Lizzie Borden Axe For It?

which won the Academy Award for Best Picture in 1931. Other Nance O'Neil films from that era include *Transgression, Ladies of Leisure,* and *The Lady of Scandal.* In later years, she also performed in radio and television.

Here is a fond first-hand reminiscence of Nance many years after her active acting career was over:

"I enjoyed first nights at the theaters--the Baldwin, Columbia, and California. It seems to me that aside from Bernhardt, the most memorable first night was when Nance O'Neil, a San Francisco girl, first appeared on the stage a star. Born Gertrude Lamson, her religious father, an auctioneer, denounced his daughter in church, for going on the stage, and asked the congregation to pray for her. She drifted away under the management of McKee Rankin, who made her a star in Australia. England also acclaimed her before she returned to her home town. . . .

Critics Lukewarm

Nance had genius that made all other actresses, except Bernhardt, seem second rate. The audience gave her curtain call after curtain call. Next morning I was surprised to find all the critics lukewarm. I said to Fremont: 'I don't know what to write.' He replied: 'Pay no attention to the other critics. Write just as you feel.' So I wrote that the San Francisco girl was a genius. She changed her program every night and I attended each performance. For a week she didn't draw, and then suddenly the theater was crowded." (*Call-Bulletin San Francisco*).

Nance O'Neil was briefly married to English actor Alfred Hickman (1872-1931), who died of a cerebral hemorrhage in April 1931. After a long career, Nance O'Neil joined him in the hereafter on the 7th of February, 1965, dying in Englewood, New Jersey. She had done countless plays, films, radio and even television, leaving behind a legacy of sixty years on the American stage and screen, favorable comparisons to Sarah Bernhardt and Eleanora Duse, and a small, but significant, part in the legend of Lizzie Borden. Most

151

Did Lizzie Borden Axe For It?

film historians believe Nance narrowly missed the lasting fame her talent should have earned her.

Miss Nance O'Neil

Talma & Co., Melbourne and Sydney, copyright

Postcard of Nance O'Neil in a Shakespearean costume from around the time she knew Lizzie--from the National Library of Australia

Did Lizzie Borden Axe For It?

II. Nance's Relationship with Lizzie

Between 1904 and 1906, Nance O'Neil was a close friend of Lizzie Borden, according to friends of Lizzie, and newspaper articles. There were rumors that they became lovers. At about the time Nance and Lizzie met, the actress was struggling to keep her career going. Her main obstacle was that she was managed by McKee Rankin, an independent actor-manager. This made her a target of the Theatrical Syndicate, which controlled many of the theaters and could influence reviews and news articles. Lizzie Borden saw her perform in her most famous roles in *Macbeth* (as Lady Macbeth) and *Hedda Gabler* (as the title character) early in 1904 prior to their initial meeting that summer. In an article for *Theatre* magazine in 1920, Nance wrote, "I have nearly always interpreted the unloved woman in the theatre, the woman crucified by the unseen, the conventional traditions." No doubt these roles appealed to Lizzie very much. Nance included herself as one of these women: "With the blind intuition that children sometimes have, I wrote in my first diary this defiant rule of life: 'Better an outlaw than not free.' We are rebels because those who govern us often, blindly, no doubt, betray us. The unloved woman is usually just such, the victim . . ." Such a remark, such a mindset, may have deeply appealed to Lizzie. It appears that Lizzie was attracted to Nance O'Neil, to a large degree, because O'Neil specialized in playing roles that Lizzie strongly identified with. I am no licensed psychologist, but I suspect from what I learned in my university courses on psychology, that Lizzie, emotionally, was a case of arrested development, never progressing beyond a certain adolescent romanticism. She may well have thought of herself as a real-life tragic anti-heroine of the type that O'Neil often portrayed. Better an outlaw than not free. That, to Lizzie, could also have meant: better a murderess than prisoner to a

Did Lizzie Borden Axe For It?

house of hate. Nance O'Neil's words: "We are rebels because those who govern us often blindly, no doubt, betray us, the unloved woman is just such, the victim . . ." may be a vague or not-so-vague reference to Lizzie herself and her strained relationship with her father, Andrew, especially the betrayal she may have felt about his siding with Abby against her. Those who believe in the incest theory that Lizzie was victimized by her father or Uncle Morse can read more into it.

The Colonial Theatre (today), where Lizzie first saw Nance O'Neil perform in 1904 and became enamoured with her--private collection

Did Lizzie Borden Axe For It?

Nance and Lizzie first met in the summer of 1904 after Lizzie first saw her on stage at the Colonial Theatre that winter and was filled with rapture over the violent intensity of Nance's performance. Nance received a note from Lizzie expressing admiration for her brilliant acting and asking permission to call on her; that was the beginning of their acquaintance. With it came a bouquet of flowers. According to one account: "Nance O'Neil received Miss Borden, as she did hundreds of others who sought her, in her dressing room at the Tremont theatre. Thereafter, however, they met at each other's homes."

They got together at a resort outside Boston, a big hotel in Tyngsboro, and later at Nance's beautiful summer home, which she called the Brindley Farm. Soon, Lizzie was lavishing gifts on her close friend and idol Nance, and the papers were calling them "inseparable." Lizzie even paid off many of Nance's ever-nagging debts brought about by her carefree, spendthrift nature and enjoyment of high living, as well as a lawsuit. Rumors in Fall River spread that Lizzie and Nance were lovers. There was even an article announcing that Lizzie was writing a play for Nance. Lizzie once financed a riotous, week-long party at Nance's home in Tyngsboro to the chagrin of its more staid puritan neighbors (*The Knowlton/Pearson Correspondence*). In June 1905, Lizzie invited Nance and her whole theatre troupe down to Maplecroft. Though she normally lived her life in reclusive peace and tranquility, there was this one notable exception. The party was lavish and included an orchestra, caterers and imported palm trees. For Lizzie, the relationship and the party were of great consequence. "I have often read that Lizzie's big party for Nance . . . was the last nail in Lizzie's coffin so far as Fall River society was concerned; and I think that it was so," wrote Victoria Lincoln in *A Private Disgrace*. Lincoln lived relatively near the aging and isolated Lizzie and was privy to all that was whispered about her during her life and after her death. Yes, Nance did in fact visit Maplecroft in June, 1905, but she confessed in an interview that she never met Emma, who had already moved out to Fairhaven in May, a month or so earlier. So it's clear that Emma didn't move as a result of any shenanigans that might have occurred at that summer party where Lizzie entertained Nance O'Neil and her theatrical company. However, to make a more interesting story no doubt, the newspapers wrote that Emma was at Maplecroft and packing her bags and leaving because of Lizzie's "wild party." What little has been reported about the relationship between Lizzie and Nance is taken from individuals who knew Lizzie. It doesn't appear to have been particularly noteworthy in the turbulent life of the actress. As one writer puts it, "O'Neil was certainly accustomed to the fervid admiration of women." Throughout her life there were also rumors about Nance having both male and female lovers. But in an age as tight-lipped about sex as the 19th and early 20th century was (let alone about same-sex relationships), it's hard to substantiate such claims.

After Lizzie's death, Nance O'Neil gave an interview about her recollections of Lizzie. Nance allowed herself to be interviewed for *The New Bedford Standard* some 4 days after Lizzie's death and she told a reporter named Minna Littmann that "Miss Borden was accustomed to come frequently to Boston, to the Bellevue, to enjoy plays and concerts and the company of a few friends, among whom Miss O'Neil recalled Mrs. Mary A. Livermore, and a brilliant woman novelist [probably Elizabeth Stuart Phelps] and her husband [of Boston], who were not merely friends, but warm companions of Lizzie Borden." Mrs. Phelps was a popular "authoress" or what was in those days sometimes dismissively called a "lady novelist". It appears that Lizzie may have been very fond of this woman's novels with their then-taboo subject-matter and feminist overtones. Lizzie and she may have become acquainted during one of Lizzie's many visits to Boston. The source that connects Mrs. Phelps directly to Lizzie is an article written just after Lizzie's death (*The Lizzie Borden Sourcebook*, p. 355) which gives her full name. In her

Did Lizzie Borden Axe For It?

interview, Nance recalled Lizzie's memorable week-long "bash" at her summer house: "Miss Borden was once a guest for a few days at her country place at Tyngsboro, not far from Lowell [Mass.]," but although Nance had high regard for Lizzie and said she didn't believe her guilty of the murders, their relationship was not a lasting one. Nance characterized herself as a poor letter-writer, so she didn't keep in touch with her infamous friend, and a busy theatre and film career would also have kept them apart. Nance described the time she knew Lizzie in this poetic way: "We were like ships that pass in the night and speak to each other in passing."

Elizabeth Stuart Phelps in later years, who was a bestselling novelist. She and her husband were close friends with Lizzie until her death in 1911--private collection

Did Lizzie Borden Axe For It?

Works cited and/or consulted:
The Boston Daily Globe, February 18, 1904
The New York Evening News, December (?), 1909
Theatre, 1920
The Knowlton/Pearson Correspondence, 1923-1930
Beth Vince, *An American Lillie Langtry*
David Beasley, The Nance O'Neil Company and the Shuberts in 1908, *The Passing Show, Shubert Archive*, Spring 1992
Cora Miranda Baggerly Older, *Call-Bulletin San Francisco*, October 10, 1955
New Bedford Standard, June 4, 1927
Hans J. Wollstein, *All Movie Guide*, 1999
Victoria Lincoln, *A Private Disgrace: Lizzie Borden By Daylight*
David Kent and Robert A. Flynn, *The Lizzie Borden Sourcebook*

Did Lizzie Borden Axe For It?

Forensic Scientist's Investigation Gets the Axe . . .
But Not The Skulls

James E. Starrs is a professor of law and forensic sciences at The George Washington University National Law Center. In 1992, Starrs and his examining colleagues went to Fall River in an effort to prove whether or not the hatchet presented at trial (handleless hatchet) was, in fact, the real murder weapon. He also wanted to exhume the skulls and bodies of the victims for his investigation but Borden relatives were against any exhumation. Aware that Andrew and Abby's skulls went missing shortly after the trial, he sampled the Borden family gravesite with radar and "located what appears to be the missing skulls 'about three feet above the rest of the remains of the Bordens,' in Fall River's Oak Grove Cemetery (Stuart, A-8). Whoever stole the skulls remains a mystery" (*Lizzie Borden Unlocked*). However, Starrs' investigation was "indefinitely postponed" because of a lack of financial support and because of the opposition to his endeavor.

It was over fifteen years ago that he abandoned his Lizzie investigation after receiving dozens of letters from "relatives" of the deceased who were protesting it. He had been eager to delve into the case and try to come up with any clues to suggest, among other things, whether the "pickax" or handless hatchet had been used in the murders. He wanted to probe the remains. He wanted to see and handle the skulls.

Did Lizzie Borden Axe For It?

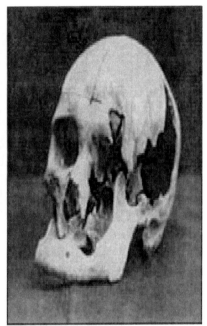

Andrew Borden's skull

Did Lizzie Borden Axe For It?

Professor James Starrs, forensic scientist who wanted to exhume the Borden skulls for analysis to determine whether the handleless hatchet was the real murder weapon--private collection

Did Lizzie Borden Axe For It?

Handleless hatchet in 1892, believed by many to have been the murder weapon--private collection

Did Lizzie Borden Axe For It?

Borden cemetery plot (today), which includes among others, Lizzie and Emma, Andrew, his first wife Sarah and second wife Abby, and Abraham, who was Andrew's father and Lizzie's grandfather--courtesy Faye Musselman

Did Lizzie Borden Axe For It?

Handleless hatchet (today)--copyright holder not known

Looking back on the aborted investigation now, Starrs shakes his head and claims, 'The worst part about it was that [the relatives] also said that they liked the mystery--the mystery being that even though she was acquitted, that everybody else thought she was guilty. They liked that. They were happy with that.' Starrs explains that he doesn't like a mystery to remain unsolved, even though his forensic digs don't always solve the case. One of his strongest opponents was a Lizzie descendant from Alexandria named Douglas Borden, who wrote a firm letter of protest against Starrs. The man now declines to make any comments, but his wife

Did Lizzie Borden Axe For It?

Joan claims that Starrs "was extremely accusatory toward Douglas. He thought he was some sort of ringleader or something.' As for the idea of exhuming the skulls some day, 'Let the dead lie in peace, regardless of who they are. Just let 'em lie,' she says.

"Starrs says he wouldn't mind being exhumed one day. 'In fact, it might be a credit for some reason as to what I've done or haven't done,' he says."

Works cited and/or consulted:
Ed Sams, *Lizzie Borden Unlocked*
Amanda Ripley, *Bone Hunter*

Did Lizzie Borden Axe For It?

Prominent Lizzie Borden expert and collector, Faye Musselman, is standing outside of the Fall River Historical Society with the infamous handleless hatchet in hand--courtesy Faye Musselman

Did Lizzie Borden Axe For It?

Were Samuel Robinsky and Hyman Lubinsky One And The Same Man?

The similarities between the man identified as Samuel Robinsky and the man we know as Hyman Lubinsky are uncanny, almost beyond coincidence. Could it really have been the same man? Let us investigate the facts.

On August 17, Emma received a letter that included the following:

"Dear Madam--You must excuse that I take the liberty in sending you these few lines. I ought to have written to you before this, as I was unable to do so, as I was travelling every day. My name is Samuel Robinsky. I am a Jewish peddler. When the fatal murder in Fall River occurred I was only a few miles from Fall River. That day, while sitting on the roadside, towards New Bedford, I met a man who was covered with blood . . ."

Jennings' attempt to track Robinsky down proved unsuccessful. He went with a seasoned investigator named J. Ryder and searched around in all the likeliest places in an attempt to find this Sam Robinsky. He talked to all the wholesale dealers in peddlers' supplies, many of them Jewish. None of them knew anybody by that name and were "willing to make affidavit that they do not believe any such man lives in this state." House-to-house inquiries were made but nobody with the last name of "Robinsky" was ever found. "Everywhere in Police Circles the Robinsky letter was considered a 'fake' pure and simple."

Did Lizzie Borden Axe For It?

Both men were Russian, both Jewish, both spoke or wrote with an accent, both presumably knew Yiddish, both said they saw something mysterious to do with the murder case, both were seemingly of similar social standing, lower-to-middle class, both were peddlers. Did Lizzie's lawyers *suspect* that Robinsky and Lubinsky were the same guy? Why does defense attorney Robinson in his trial closing arguments mispronounce Lubinsky "Lobinsky" over and over? A Freudian slip? So if Hyman Lubinsky did use the alias of Samuel Robinsky to write the letter, what would have been his reason to use an alias? In his letter he seems very afraid of being implicated in the murder and tells Emma not to tell the police what he writes to her, as he fears that they would arrest him. Did he ride his buggy out all the way to New Bedford that day?

According to his letter, Robinsky didn't know about the murder when he saw his blood-smeared man, and of course neither did Lubinsky when he spotted a woman coming slowly from the Borden barn at around 11 o'clock. Was it Lubinsky's fear of being implicated in the crime that caused him to write the Robinsky letter under alias, if he did indeed write it? Were they one and the same "chap" as they say? We know Robinsky supposedly disappeared and all attempts to track him down failed--but if the letter was written under Lubinsky's alias and Robinsky didn't exist, then of course no one "disappeared." Could he really have been Hyman Lubinsky but was too afraid to fess up to it because he had allowed the blood-smeared man to get away and dreaded a public backlash against him because of it? Especially since he was a foreigner and would have feared a xenophobic public and police. Was "Samuel Robinsky" just an alias of Hyman Lubinsky? Was Lubinsky the real author of that letter? If they are two different men, then the coincidences are startling. *Both* are Russian, *both* Jewish, *both* travelling peddlers by trade, *both* having a foreigner's difficulty with English, *both* saw something potentially very mysterious to do with the Borden tragedy. It makes you think. Most likely of all, the

Did Lizzie Borden Axe For It?

similarities are just a big coincidence . . . but maybe not.

Works cited and/or consulted:
The Witness Statements for the Lizzie Borden Murder Case
A letter addressed to "Miss Emma Borden", dated August 17, 1892

NOTE: Emma received a letter addressed to "Miss Emma Borden" and purporting to be written in Waltham, Massachusetts, August 17, 1892, *just one day after* Joseph Lemay allegedly saw a blood-smeared stranger sitting with a hatchet on his lap. Robinsky's letter seems to describe the same man: "on the roadside, towards New Bedford, I met a man who was covered with blood . . ." and whose physical appearance resembles many of the accounts of a stranger who was reportedly seen near the Borden house on 92 Second Street on the morning of the murders.

Did Lizzie Borden Axe For It?

Whose Blood Was In That Pail?

Anything to do with menstrual blood was shocking and improper and Knowlton didn't pursue it at the trial. Damn Victorian propriety! There are people firmly convinced that a pail filled with bloodied cloths found in the cellar was involved in the murders and used by the murderer in his/her clean-up. There was, we know, a blood-stained cloth or handkerchief found on the guest-room bed at the scene of Abby's murder, but not Andrew's. There was a folded coat found under him on the sofa which had blood-smears and the hatchet may have been wiped into it. However, the murderer would still have needed to wipe his/her bloodied hands and other parts, presumably, after the second murder. *If there was a menstrual "bucket" in the kitchen (and there was) why was there also a pail with bloodied rags in the cellar?* The killer wiped the blade after Abby's murder and left the cloth there. In Andrew's case, the weapon was probably wiped into the coat found under his body, therefore there was no tell-tale blood trail of the murder weapon which there otherwise most certainly would have been.

If Lizzie was the killer, Bridget probably saved her ass when it comes to the menstrual stuff--she would have known or at least suspected that the bloodied rags in the cellar weren't from Lizzie's period. How do we know this? Well, aside from the fact that Bridget refused to sleep in the same house with Lizzie and opted to stay at the house of a neighbor, Southard Miller, there was *already* a menstrual bucket in the kitchen, so why the bloody pail in the cellar? There is also a very compelling reason why Bridget may have suspected Lizzie was the killer. It comes from *The Witness Statements*, p. 28. Lizzie's period ended Wednesday, yet Bridget couldn't account for what looked like "small towels, they were covered with blood, and in a pail half-filled with water, and in the wash cellar." According to Lizzie, this bloody pail had been there *for three or four days*. But when Officer Medley asked Bridget about it, she contradicted Lizzie, saying "she had *not* noticed the pail *until that day* [day of the murders]" and added that it couldn't have been there before because she would have seen it and put it in the wash. To put it simply, that pail and the bloodied cloths were implicated in the murders. Think about it: Bridget says that bloody pail wasn't there until that day of the murders (Thursday). But Lizzie's period ended on Wednesday! Therefore, since the pail was there only on Thursday, the blood could not have come from Lizzie's period which ended Wednesday. Apparently then, it was used by the killer to wash the blood-stains off of herself (or himself).

Works cited and/or consulted:
The Superior Court Trial Transcript, Vol. 1, pp. 1-988
The Witness Statements for the Lizzie Borden Murder Case

Did Lizzie Borden Axe For It?

The Question of an Outside Killer

The biggest question in this whole Lizzie mystery has always been: who killed the Bordens? Some are convinced that it was Lizzie, and Lizzie alone, who perpetrated the murders. Still others believe that Lizzie had an accomplice. Then there are also the Lizzie defenders, apologists, and sympathizers who believe that Lizzie is innocent; they look to other alternatives for an answer to this most infamous crime in the annals of American justice. The specific individuals who have been suspected of the murders have been countless, ranging from the plausible to the unlikely to the downright absurd, and they include the likes of Emma Borden, Doctor Bowen, even two young boys "Me and Brownie". And a fair amount of books and articles have been written exploring these theories. It sometimes seems like the only people who haven't been suspected of the murders were the victims themselves! I won't take up the incredible task of evaluating each and every one of these suspects and the theories surrounding them, but what I *will* do is use the facts to explore how possible or impossible it is for any outside killer to have murdered the Bordens. First the theories.

David Kent in *Forty Whacks* points out that up in the hayloft of the barn, the hay was pressed down giving the impression that two bodies had layed there. He theorized that a killer(s) could have spent the night in the loft on the eve before the murders and then snuck into the house a few paces away the next morning. There are also those who argue that a hired murderer could have admitted

172

himself or been admitted right into the house the night before. John Morse testified that he heard someone come in through the front door late Wednesday night and go up into Lizzie's room. He couldn't see who it was, only heard it. Theoretically, the killer could then have remained concealed in Lizzie's room the whole night and while everyone went downstairs for breakfast in the morning. Then when Abby went upstairs again to put on fresh pillow-cases, the killer spots her and goes for the kill; remains hidden in the house and then commits the second murder. Another theory is that a murderer could also have come home with Bridget the night before and stayed upstairs with her. There were two bedrooms up in the third floor attic--Bridget's and the one that Morse apparently lived in years earlier for an entire year. This would mean, of course, that Bridget would have been an accomplice also. It's also possible to theorize that Lizzie or anyone in on the murder, like Bridget or Morse, could have let the murderer in through any one of the three possible entrances to the house at any time when the coast was clear on Wednesday night or Thursday morning. Also, the side door was unhooked when Bridget went outside to vomit for 10-15 minutes Thursday morning, and from 9:30 AM onwards it was intermittently left unhooked. This would, presumably, have allowed for a murderer to slip inside and do the deadly deeds. How likely are these various possibilities? An examination of the facts can tell us.

At the trial, Thomas Barlow testified that he and his friend Everett Brown ("Me and Brownie") had been playing in the hay of the loft, looking to see if the killer was hiding there; so it's very reasonable to assume that those two "body impressions" were made by these two boys rather than a killer(s) sleeping there on the eve before the murders. Furthermore, the barn door was habitually kept locked to keep out thieves, so no killer could have gotten in and slept up there anyway. The person Morse heard come inside through the front door Wednesday evening was almost certainly Lizzie herself, who had been visiting at Alice Russell's house from 7 o'clock to about 9. And there is no evidence at all that a potential murderer (hired hitman) was let into the house on Wednesday night and hidden, poised to strike at the right opportunity, which happened to be the following morning. Nor is there the slightest trace of evidence to show that an assailant was let in or sneaked into the house when Bridget was outside in the yard vomiting, or at any other time that morning. She herself claimed to have seen no one, and *no one* else saw anyone on the Borden property either.

It's established that there were three separate entrances to the house--the cellar door out back, the side or screen door, and the front door. That's not including the windows of course, but some (if not all) of them had screens. And again, no knowledge of a suspect trying something so bold as to crawl inside a window in broad daylight even if there were no screen. On the morning of the murders, the cellar door and front door were both locked from the inside the whole time according to Bridget and the police officers who checked them, so no intruder could have gotten in those ways on his own. The screen door at the side porch was also hooked, but only part of the time. As George D. Robinson says at the trial in his *Closing Arguments for the Defense*: "The side screen door, gentlemen, was unfastened from about 9 o'clock to 10:45 or 11. That is when Bridget was washing windows and about the house and around the premises in the way she said she was. Now if that door wasn't locked, gentlemen, Lizzie wasn't locked in and everybody else wasn't locked out. You know [at 9:30] Bridget said to Lizzie, 'You needn't lock the door, I am going to be round here.' There is no doubt about it. Then there was a perfect entrance to that house by that rear screen door, wasn't there? And when the person got in, all he had to do was to avoid meeting Bridget and Lizzie." But even if the assailant wasn't spotted by Bridget outside from about 9:00 AM, could he have eluded detection by Lizzie inside? And did he commit the first murder after 9:30 when the screen door was unhooked? The answer both times is most probably "no." The sound and logical conclusion about the time of Abby's murder is this: she died a little after 9 because the only task she had left to do in the guest-room was to slip on a few clean pillow-cases, yet she never came down and was never heard from again alive; it only takes a few moments to change a few slips. As far as avoiding Lizzie, this is impossible when you realize that the murderer couldn't have gotten to Abby through the backstairs, and to get to Abby he would *have to have* encountered Lizzie on the first floor, either seen or heard by her, since she was in the kitchen and dining-room almost the whole period during that time. Also, Robinson's estimate of when the side door was unfastened is incorrect. It was really a shorter span of time--from 9:30 to about 10:20 or 30 when Bridget had finished doing the windows from the outside and had begun to clean them from the inside. We know that by about 10:45 the side door was already locked and hooked because Andrew tried to get in that way and couldn't. He had to be admitted in through the front door by Bridget.

It's absolutely amazing when you realize that even if by some fluke an outside killer got in unseen by Bridget or anyone, Lizzie was in the kitchen reading a magazine or in the dining-room ironing. One could *not* get to the guest-room through the backstairs because the door between Andrew/Abby's and Lizzie's bedroom was kept locked at all times; there was also a heavy bureau or chest-of-drawers on the elder Borden's side of that door that kept it out of use. So, because the backstairs was not an option for getting at Abby, the killer would have *needed to* pass by Lizzie, and as a result would have spotted her and/or been spotted by her at one point or another because she would have been in the kitchen or dining-room at the bottom floor of the house at that time. It's established that Lizzie was on the bottom part of that house within the time span that it is believed Abby died. How could the killer have made it past Lizzie completely unseen or completely unheard? Due to the obstruction of the big bureau and locked doors up the rear stairs, the intruder would have had *no alternative but* to walk right pass Lizzie in the kitchen to proceed to the front stairs to get at Abby in the guest-room, or would have to have gone through the door between the kitchen and the sitting-room while Lizzie was preoccupied in the dining-room, but that door was not in use; it was kept closed (or locked) most of the time because of the heat from the kitchen stove nearby. In the summer, it was closed to keep the sitting-room comfortable. But even if the intruder used that door successfully, Lizzie would be expected to have at least heard him go through the sitting-room, if not seen him. If some person came in off the street with murder on his mind, it makes sense that he would have first encountered Lizzie and killed her! But that didn't happen. Therefore, the question must be asked: did Lizzie do it or conspire with the killer?

The facts are clear. Due to the *complete* lack of evidence, it's unlikely and unproven that there was a hired hitman admitted into the house on the eve or day of the murders; and it's just as unlikely and unproven that an unhired intruder did the deeds based on the near impossibility of his committing the crimes all undetected by Bridget and Lizzie. But *even if* he miraculously managed this nearly impossible feat of murder(s) unnoticed, his next incredible challenge was to make it out of the house and away without being seen and without getting caught. Yet, a careful analysis of the *Trial Transcript* and *Witness Statements* of the Lizzie case shows that of all the individuals from the various houses, properties, streets and vantage-points, no one saw any potential killer. Sure, people like Mrs. Manley and Dr. Handy saw people either standing on the street or walking down the street suspiciously near the Borden house, but nothing to suggest a murderer escaping. "Dr. Handy's wild-eyed man" was later identified as a mill worker named Michael Graham. Likewise, the other mysterious types were similarly identified or otherwise dismissed as implausible suspects. Page 35 of *The Fall River Tragedy* tells us that Lizzie's own lawyer Andrew Jennings

Did Lizzie Borden Axe For It?

immediately after the murders himself admitted: "Then for a man to enter, commit the deed and escape without being discovered, would be a remarkable combination of circumstances." Along with the fact that there is zip, zilch, zero evidence that any suspicious character came into the house either the evening before or the morning of the murders, there is no real proof that any outside killer made a get-away either. Thomas Bowles, a resident at the Churchill house next door, said he would've seen anyone come through that yard--didn't; Lucy Collett testified that she would have seen anyone come out the back yard over the Borden fence--didn't; several men positioned all over the Crowe yard would have seen anyone in that yard--didn't; various residents along Second Street and Third Street would be expected to have seen a killer escaping too--didn't. They were all questioned. *None* of them saw anyone. It may be so that no one saw John Morse actually leave the Borden house at 8:45 or 50 AM, but he *was* seen along his itinerary and his nephew/niece, the Emerys, sealed his alibi. Yet isn't it interesting that not one soul ever saw or heard this so-called Outside Killer either come into the house, commit the deeds, or escape. No one noticed any of it, *nothing*. Either he was invisible, or extremely lucky, or . . . !

Works cited and/or consulted:
David Kent, *Forty Whacks: New Evidence in the Life and Legend of Lizzie Borden*
The Superior Court Trial Transcript Vol. 1, pp. 1-988
Edwin H. Porter, *The Fall River Tragedy*
The Inquest Upon the Deaths of Andrew J. and Abby D. Borden, August 9 - 11, 1892, Volume I & II

Did Lizzie Borden Axe For It?

NOTE #1: From Lizzie's own inquest testimony: except for a very brief trip to the cellar, she claims to have been in the kitchen or dining-room the whole time when the alleged killer must have snuck into the house and struck Abby, but she says she saw or heard nothing out of the ordinary. Furthermore, the killer had to walk past her to get to the front hall and up the front stairs to kill Abby, but Lizzie claims she didn't see/hear him. If she didn't do it, why didn't she see or at least hear the murderer?

NOTE #2: At the time of the murders, the door between Lizzie's and Andrew/Abby's bedroom was permanently kept locked and there was a heavy bureau behind the door on the Andrew/Abby bedroom side; also, the rear-stairs door to the Borden bedroom was habitually locked; that means a killer would definitely have had to go past Lizzie on the ground floor to get to Abby through the front stairs.

NOTE #3: The testimony of Collet, Desrosier, Mrs. Bowen, Bowles, etc shows that no potential murderer was seen. Allegedly a woman named Ellen Eagan saw a man on the pathway in front of the porch steps of the Borden side entrance in a gray overcoat, of pale complexion, holding a coarse homespun bag; but this story comes second or third hand and many years after the fact, included in Arnold Brown's *Lizzie Borden: The Legend, The Truth, The Final Chapter*; it has never been substantiated in any way and is commonly believed to be highly questionable, if not an outright fabrication by Brown.

NOTE #4: John Morse had an airtight alibi. Mrs. Horace Kingsley of Weybosset Street saw Morse on the same street that morning. Morse also approached a gentleman stranger (Henry W. Clarke) on Weybosset Street, who later identified him on sight in a letter to Arthur Phillips dated March 28, 1938

Did Lizzie Borden Axe For It?

The Latest On The William "Billy" Borden Story

In 1991, Arnold R. Brown published a book titled *Lizzie Borden: The Legend, The Truth, The Final Chapter* which he claimed to have put together using the notes of a Henry Hawthorne. These notes consisted of so-called remembrances of Henry Hawthorne from when he was a boy working for a farmer named Bill Borden; Hawthorne wrote these remembrances down when he was 89 years old. Brown's book alleges that these notes reveal Henry Hawthorne and Ellen Eagan, together, were able to identify the real killer of Andrew and Abby Borden as Bill Borden, who Brown claims was an illegitimate son of Andrew driven to murder because Andrew refused to include him in his will. Neither claim has ever been proven, either that Andrew had an illegitimate son or that he ever had a will. None was ever filed in probate court while Andrew lived. Lewis "Pete" Peterson was a relative of Hawthorne who lent Hawthorne's notes to Brown for his book. Peterson died a few years ago, and Arnold Brown is also deceased.

Len Rebello tells me: "He ['Pete'] was a great person to know and was instrumental in getting information on Henry Hawthorne. I spoke with him at the Borden house to tell him of all the research I uncovered on Hawthorne and Bill Borden. He listened, but said, 'I don't know anything about that [research]. His [Hawthorne's] facts and dates of events were proved to be incorrect.' I also met Pete at the 1992 conference and spent the day with him. He was very angry at Arnold Brown, saying that he changed Henry's story. I interviewed two nieces of Henry and both laughed when they read Brown's book and their uncle's notes. They never remembered their uncle speaking of or telling stories about Lizzie Borden or Billy Borden. They simply laughed. You see, Henry, in later life, embellished his stories quite a bit. . . . I believe 'Pete' Peterson who said Brown twisted the story, and reportedly, the notes or letters he gave to Brown. You see, he invented his storyline and made all the pieces fit."

So, it appears that Henry Hawthorne, in order to make himself interesting, made up or embellished on his story about Billy Borden, and then on top of that, author Arnold Brown embellished on Hawthorne's embellishments! Given this, it's very likely that the account about Hawthorne overhearing Bill Borden talking to his hatchet and saying: "you know my father [Andrew] should have married my mother when he married that fat sow [Abby]. You know, and you were there when they died"--it's likely this story is false. Also, the claim that Ellen Eagan encountered a scary strange young man on the Borden property on the morning of the murders is highly unlikely also, since the *Fall River Daily Herald* and the *Boston Herald* of the same day both explain that it was the Kelly yard that she went into, not the Borden yard, and she herself as far as we know never said anything about seeing this man, either on the witness stand or in private.

Let us hope that the legend of Billy Borden has at last been exposed, the truth revealed, and the final chapter ended.

Works cited and/or consulted:
Arnold R. Brown, Lizzie Borden: *The Legend, The Truth, The Final Chapter*

Did Lizzie Borden Axe For It?

Boston Herald, August 11, 1892
Fall River Daily Herald, August 11, 1892

Taunton State Asylum for the Criminally Insane, where Arnold Brown alleged that Billy Borden was a patient before and after the murders--private collection

Did Lizzie Borden Axe For It?

Mary Livermore: An Important Ally

There's no evidence that Lizzie was a feminist or "suffragette" as was the term in those days (Nance O'Neil in the interview just after her death referred to her as "old-fashioned"), but there is no doubt that Lizzie enjoyed the feminist literature of women like Elizabeth Stuart Phelps and the pro-women plays of Henrik Ibsen, and she was inspired by such women and ideals. Indeed, many such women took up her cause during the trial, one of the more prominent of them being Mrs. Mary Livermore.

Mary A. R. Livermore (1820-1905) was an American journalist, philanthropist, and lecturer during the nineteenth century. She was a key organizer for the United States Sanitary Commission during the Civil War. Afterwards, she turned her energies to women's rights and became a prominent leader of the woman suffrage and temperance movements, and a popular lecturer on social reform. She was the only female reporter at Lincoln's nomination. After the Civil War she was active in both temperance, suffrage, and abolitionist movements.

In early adulthood, she observed the way that slaves on the plantation were treated and this turned her into a strong opponent of US slavery and a steadfast supporter of Lincoln in the 1860 presidential election. In 1868 she organized the Chicago Woman Suffrage Convention and established *The Agitator*, a popular feminist journal, to advocate temperance reform and woman suffrage.

Did Lizzie Borden Axe For It?

Mary Livermore was also one of the leaders of the Women's Christian Temperance Union (WCTU), and when she learned of Lizzie, who was also a member of that same organization in trouble, she stood by her unwaveringly. After all, Lizzie's birth mother Sarah Morse Borden had been a close friend of hers; furthermore, Mrs. Livermore was a woman of strong religious faith, and she could not fathom another Christian woman who she imagined to be much like herself committing such a ghastly double murder.

Lizzie was personally visited by her in Taunton jail and received her sympathy and condolences. Some of the press mocked at this and questioned whether she was over-empathizing with Lizzie and forgetting about the victims, who they reminded their readers may very well have been murdered by Lizzie.

The old Bristol County Jail, better known as Taunton jail, where Lizzie spent almost ten months pending her trial. The building was demolished in 1970

Did Lizzie Borden Axe For It?

Ash Street Jail in New Bedford, where Lizzie was held during her trial--courtesy Ron Rolo

Did Lizzie Borden Axe For It?

Leading Massachusetts suffragette Mary Livermore was Lizzie's most influential supporter and defender outside of the courtroom. Thanks in large part to her, many women backed Lizzie during the trial--from the Library of Congress

Did Lizzie Borden Axe For It?

The Providence Journal of Sunday, June 25, 1893 printed *The Borden Case, How Public Opinion in Boston Regards the Verdict, Mrs. Mary A. Livermore Rises to the Occasion*: "How much popular sympathy Mrs. Livermore and the rest expect to win I do not pretend to say. I have talked with many women about this case, and almost all of them agree that the accusation was by no means incredible. 'Of course a woman could have done it!'--that is their opinion. Whether or not they are mistaken as to the capacities of their sex let others decide. I think, on the whole, that the public here have experienced a feeling of relief at the verdict. Few go to such lengths as Mrs. Livermore. But even those who suspected Miss Borden all along see that the evidence is not conclusive. . . . The belief that Miss Borden herself ought not to rest content with the verdict is well nigh universal. Although the jury could not see their way clear to render any other verdict on the evidence submitted, the importance of finding the real criminal is not diminished. Perhaps this would be a useful outlet for the energies of Mrs. Livermore and her friends. It would be better than forming a Society for the Admiration of Lizzie Borden, which is the usual Boston way . . ."

Works cited and/or consulted:
New Bedford Standard, June 4, 1927
Charles A. Howe, *Mary and Daniel Livermore*
Patrick Chadwick, *Mary A. Livermore Biography*
Leonard Rebello, *Lizzie Borden: Past & Present*
The Providence Journal, June 25, 1893

Did Lizzie Borden Axe For It?

The Robinson Papers

The Fall River Historical Society is now transcribing and will be publishing the 600 or so documents of the Hilliard Papers some time in the future. Rufus B. Hilliard was the city marshal at the time of the Borden murders and he received many letters from people confessing to the murders; also letters of praise about how he and the police were conducting themselves, and letters of criticism, a few of them very bitter and harsh. These will all be published under one volume. The Knowlton Papers have already been published in hardcover. But what will *not* be awaiting publication (now, or as far as we know, ever) is the Robinson Papers. George Dexter Robinson was Lizzie Borden's key attorney at her trial. It was in no small part due to him and his cunning arguments that Lizzie was acquitted. The documents pertaining to this collection are kept at the law firm located in Springfield, Mass., which still bears his name. The long and short of it is, the Robinson firm refuses to disclose the documents. Even now, more than 115 years later, the papers remain hidden from public view, even though they are probably the last great body of fresh historical evidence on one of the most sensational episodes in legal history. In *The Borden Murder Mystery: In Defense of Lizzie Borden*, p. 7, Arthur S. Phillips writes that our knowledge of all things Lizzie "has been limited to such facts as were evidenced at the trial, plus those disclosed by the prosecution and those revealed by press investigation. *The mass of documents and other evidence collected by the defense have never been disclosed* or discussed, due to the fact that until the recent death of Miss Borden, *their secrecy was, in the opinion of Mr. Jennings, important to her defense.*"

Bruce Lyon is administrator at the Robinson firm, and according to him, "the papers have been catalogued and placed in protective document folders" and the collection includes newspaper clippings and other materials that were publicly available. It also includes a lot more material, he said, all of which is privileged. It's possible that even Bridget's Inquest testimony currently resides in the Robinson files in Springfield. On Friday, June 16, 1893, the 11th day of the Trial, Robinson stood there in the courtroom holding in his hand Bridget's Inquest testimony which he had the stenographer Annie White read from. But this testimony has since disappeared for good.

Around the time of the 100th anniversary of the murders, in 1992, the firm consulted with the Board of Bar Overseers, the agency that oversees the conduct of lawyers. The board informally advised that not only does the attorney-client privilege bar the firm from releasing the papers, it prevents the firm from disclosing the nature of what it holds. Supposedly the files are in a storage room on the 16th floor locked in a 5 drawer file cabinet, but that's all we know about them. "Speculation is that the files might contain letters between Lizzie and Robinson; letters between Robinson and other lawyers involved in the case; Robinson's notes, both strategic preparations and documenting how the trial progressed; and other documents relating to testimony at the trial and preliminary proceedings. Few expect to find anything directly incriminating Lizzie, such as a signed confession."

As early as 1992 Professor Jules Ryckebusch, founding publisher of the *Lizzie Borden Quarterly*, made an effort to effect the release of the Robinson files. "Certainly client-attorney confidentiality is valuable, but I think 100 years is a fair amount of time," said Ryckebusch. "They're a very important part of history."

Did Lizzie Borden Axe For It?

They are also, according to many, a big missing piece of the Lizzie Borden puzzle. A reply from the law firm advised him that the Bar Counsel and the Board of Bar Overseers decided that a release of these materials would be a violation of the various rules and canons of ethics regarding confidentiality of client materials. They went on to say that while the Bar Counsel agreed that the materials are historically interesting, their office was faced with ethical and legal principles that prohibited them from discussing and divulging what information they have. Apparently the situation has not improved with the passage of years. Arnold Rosenfeld, a lawyer for the Massachusetts Board of Bar Overseers, cautioned the firm about making the papers public. The board enforces ethical standards among lawyers. "The duty to protect confidential information survives death in Massachusetts," he said in an interview. "That's clear. There's case law." Jeffrey McCormick, a partner at the firm of Robinson, Donovan, Madden & Berry who has browsed through the drawers of papers, refused to say what the files hold. "Historically, they can be interesting to read," McCormick said. Then, with a faint grin, he added, "I'm not saying that there's some smoking gun in there." This last bastion of hope for a major revelation of the crime mystery appears stalled in time. But there is hope. John C. Corrigan, a fine Lizzie scholar who recently passed away ("rest in peace"), and who taught at the law schools at Harvard and Roger Williams University cleverly stated, "At some point, the legitimate claims of history probably outweigh embarrassing somebody 300 years after her death." If the Robinson files contain something that should be a matter of public record (like Bridget's undisclosed inquest testimony), then it shouldn't be against attorney/client privilege to release it, right? In fact, if it was there and was the only existing copy of a historic document that was a matter of public record and was connected with the legal history of Mass., wouldn't they almost be *obliged* to release it? Telling the public if it is in there is the very least they could do. Leonard Rebello, author of *Lizzie Borden, Past*

Did Lizzie Borden Axe For It?

& Present, believes: "The Robinson papers will be revealed one day, despite the Supreme Court ruling. It will take a panel of experts and the Robinson firm to request the court to release them for 'historical' purposes with the understanding that the papers will be reviewed by the experts and Robinson firm. The person in charge of those papers was a former history teacher and historians, at least from my viewpoint, do not like to shield historical documents. Perhaps the court would release those papers that were public documents, like Bridget's inquest testimony. I do believe the papers will be released, but [it] will be done very carefully. In the [Vince] Foster case, family members are still living while in Lizzie's case they are all dead. A good case can be made by the right legal team to release the papers." A very high-profile attorney could make it into a well-publicized event and the Robinson firm might feel pressured by media attention to unleash the Robinson files for their importance as criminal history documents. These files today have much more historical significance than legal significance since all the participants of the Borden trial are dead and any decision to release the files would have no direct bearing on any one of them. But a Supreme Court ruling is a Supreme Court ruling, very hard to overturn. The argument about "ethics regarding confidentiality of attorney/client" just doesn't hold water with many Borden experts and historians. If anything, we have an ethical duty to get to the truth of this case. Lizzie was legally acquitted of all charges, but in most people's hearts she was guilty. Also, in many people's hearts she was innocent. Who's right? The Robinson Papers probably shed some light on the answer to this.

How does one go about overturning a Supreme Court ruling? Signatures from common laymen and women won't be enough. It will require a high-profile attorney, as well as Borden historians and various other scholars to bring forth a powerful case for their release. The argument would have to be that the Robinson files are of important legal and historical significance and that besides, all the participants in the case are all deceased. Information at the Pentagon is (or has been) routinely de-classified, and that's stuff from World War 2. Lizzie is 1893. I think Rebello would qualify as one of those experts who could be used to argue the case for their release. But such a formidable body of legal, criminal, and history experts would first need to be organized and assembled. But that's costly and time-consuming. Who will put the wheels in spin? Anybody? We'll have to wait and see.

It isn't just curiosity and the sake of historical accuracy. Look at anything that's been published on the Borden case, including the websites. Some of them support the belief that the Borden case is the top murder case in history--because of its unique mystery elements and because it was not solved. If there had been no controversy around the verdict in the Borden case, it would still have been hot at the time but would have gradually receded to obscurity like so many other sensational Victorian murders. But it is this great controversy about Lizzie's innocence/guilt that keeps this story so alive. Lord knows there have been plenty of TV documentaries about the case, many books, and countless websites. Mr. McCormick's claim that there is no "smoking gun" may very well be right or it may not, *but* in either case what he says is relative--what is not a "smoking gun" to him might be to contemporary Borden authors like Rebello or Masterton. It all depends on the specifics of the documents. If Jeffrey McCormick is only superficially acquainted with the Borden case, then what he's telling us is "there's no confession note." Well, we already guessed that. But given all the mountains of info some of us have read/studied on the case, these documents of the Robinson Papers would be viewed in a whole other perspective by us than they might have been by him. We'd be able to compare information in them to information we now have and see if there are discrepancies, and certain things that may at first have seemed inconsequential may suddenly become important pieces of the puzzle. Or we may at least get new insights into Lizzie's relationship with her lawyers, things that she or they may have been concerned about, etc. It is likely there would also be exculpatory evidence in Lizzie's favor.

The argument for the Robinson files' historical significance is compelling and so are arguments in favor of their release. The Lizzie story to us is what Jack the Ripper is to the Brits, it's our most infamous Victorian murder story. If it were just any other Victorian murder, then one could make an argument about how this may remain privileged information, since its historical importance would be lacking. *But* given the prominence of the case and the intense interest the Bordenite community has for this case, an interest which continues to grow, these may be files very important both to the study of law history, criminal justice, not to mention solving the greatest mystery in American criminology of the Victorian era. It may be the missing piece to a puzzle which might otherwise become complete. All participants of the trial are long dead. The Selected Journals of Canadian author L. M. Montgomery are being published only after the people who knew her have passed away. The publication date of the fourth and final volume of these journals was delayed for this reason. But those who were involved in the Borden case and trial are *long* dead. The release of these files can have no directly positive/negative ethical effect period, one may logically argue. Many descendants of the people who were involved in the case are hardly aware of it, and even with the few who are, it can be nothing more than a little gossipy fact to brag about during Sunday brunch when friends are over. The reasonable argument is that the Papers' release after the passing of over a hundred years would have little or no detrimental effect on the attorney/client privilege, and no effect what-so-ever on any descendants.

Yes it was a Supreme Court decision. Yes, it would be tough to overturn. But we have a good case here.

Did Lizzie Borden Axe For It?

* * * * *

Some years ago, I was pleased to take part in an organized and collective effort to solicit a release and/or examination of the Robinson Papers. Jeffrey McCormick said that they frequently get phone requests, emails and letters, requesting release of the files. "Those letters generally go unanswered, though they are kept on file." But our effort did receive a brief, though polite, response. The firm remains *firm* in its position:

May 28, 2001

Mr. Jeffrey L. McCormick
Attorney At Law
Robinson, Donovan, Madden & Barry, P.C.
1500 Main Street
Springfield, Massachusetts 01115

Dear Mr. McCormick:

This letter is written in reference to the undisclosed Robinson files of the Lizzie Borden case that are in the possession of your firm. I am writing on behalf of the historians and researchers of the Borden case, identified below.

Various articles have stated that the Bar of Overseers has advised your firm to not release the contents of this file because it would infringe upon the lawyer-client privilege. We also understand that you would be hesitant to release them because future clients would view this action as jeopardizing your credibility on their behalf. Also, a recent Supreme Court decision indicated that the lawyer-client privilege was effective even after death. Although there are no direct descendants of Lizzie Borden to inquire of there are very distant relations living today.

All this not withstanding, on the possibility that the Supreme Court ruling was advisory and not an edict, and that perhaps the Borden case, being over a hundred years old, would not be governed by the ruling, we would like to know if your firm might be amenable to releasing the documents for historical reasons. The following questions are asked so that we might known what the present position of your firm is in regard to the issues surrounding these files:

1. If the file contains the inquest testimony of Bridget Sullivan, could this be released since it is a public document of which no other known copy exists? This is a vital piece of information that the Robinson files might be the only repository for.

2. Would the firm release at least those documents in the file which were not lawyer-client related, such as heretofore unpublished photographs or the will of Andrew Borden?

3. Would the firm be willing to release the file contents, either on their own or by requesting the court, to a qualified assemblage of historical authorities? As a precedent the Knowlton and Jennings papers have already been published for historical research.

4. With all due respect to the Bar of Overseers position, is there any way that at the very least a list of the documents residing in the file could be made public?

Did Lizzie Borden Axe For It?

5. Of what value is confidentiality if both the client, attorney and all persons involved in the case are now dead and no one at all is able to read or use the information contained therein?

Thank you very much for your attention to the issues raised here and I hope that you will respond to this request for information at your convenience. We are extremely interested in the Lizzie Borden case and its value to American history.

Sincerely,

Carol Pedersen

Fritz Adilz, Stockhom, Sweden
Sherry Chapman, Detroit, Michigan
Terence Duniho, Providence, R.I.
David Rehak, B.C., Canada
Robert Gutowski, Jackson Heights, N.Y.
Harold Widdows, Spartanburg, S.C.
Jon Daehnke, Portland, Oregon
Debbie Borden, New Paltz, New York
Sue LaShomb, New Paltz, New York
Carl Paiva, Muskegon, Michigan
Mona Holland, Des Moines, Iowa

Did Lizzie Borden Axe For It?

June 19, 2001

RE: Lizzie Borden Documentation

Dear Ms. Pedersen:

Thank you for your letter of June 3. Regretfully, I must advise that the firm's position as to the release or discussion of any documents regarding the Borden case has been set for some time. None of the documentation is going to be released or discussed. Further, we are unwilling to allow for the review of any of the documentation by any individual.

Very truly yours,

Jeffrey L. McCormick

Works cited and/or consulted:
Arthur Sherman Phillips, *The Borden Murder Mystery: In Defense of Lizzie Borden*
Paul Edward Parker, *Lizzy Borden's Legal Papers Found*, *Providence Journal-Bulletin*, 1998
Jeff Donn, Lizzie Borden Papers Stay Sealed, *The Associated Press*, 1999

Did Lizzie Borden Axe For It?

Newfound Lizzie Letter

Here we have a copy of a note written by Lizzie, which was obtained by a Miss Dinsmoor (not Densmore, by the way). Miss Dinsmoor also may have known Miss Borden quite well and apparently kept the note for the sake of history. We are indebted to her for it, as it's the latest, and perhaps last, surviving letter written by Lizzie Borden which we have or know of. The letter was kindly sent to me by a fine gentleman from El Paso, Texas who works as a courtroom bailiff, named Joseph Robert Calamia. I then brought it to the attention of my friend and colleague in all things Lizzie, Faye Musselman, as well as to the Fall River Historical Society.

Incidentally, this Miss Dinsmoor was the grandmother of a former judge, and it was this Judge Robert Dinsmoor who was good enough to allow Mr. Calamia to make a copy of the note for my book. Lizzie's handwriting can be a little hard to read, and he has done a good job of transcribing it from the original.

The note has "Maplecroft, 306 French St." as the return address, and reads:

"C/O A. Stomell & Co. The toilet case came to me safely and is very satisfactory. I have a fitted suitcase with toilet articles in white, can you put a blue (bluish?) B. on each piece if they were sent? Very Truly Yours, Miss L. A. Borden, July 29, 1912"

Lizzie is apparently writing some company to let them know that she received a toilet case (make-up case, in today's terms). She is also indicating that she has some type of matching

Did Lizzie Borden Axe For It?

suitcase with toilet articles in white. She is probably referring to hair brushes, combs, and things of that nature. She is asking this company if they can print the capital letter "B" (in blue?) onto the toilet articles in her matching suitcase, obviously for her last name of Borden.

She wrote this note just ten days after turning fifty-two, and twenty years after her famous double murder trial involving her father and stepmother. The history student may also notice that this note was written just three-and-a-half months after the sinking of HMS Titanic.

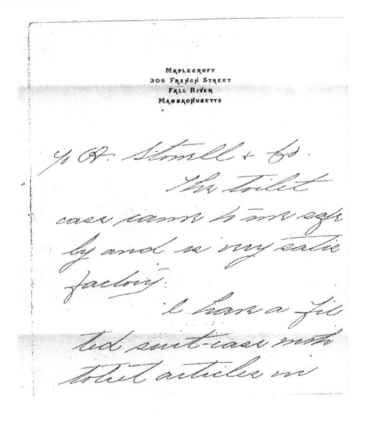

Newly discovered letter written by Lizzie Borden, page 1-- courtesy Robert Dinsmoor

Did Lizzie Borden Axe For It?

Newly discovered letter written by Lizzie Borden, page 2--courtesy Robert Dinsmoor

Did Lizzie Borden Axe For It?

While in Rome on her European tour two years before the murders, Lizzie fell in love with this painting, Raphael's Sistine Madonna. It's not known whether Lizzie ever longed for motherhood, or marriage for that matter--private collection

Did Lizzie Borden Axe For It?

St. Peter's Cathedral (today), the most grand and beautiful cathedral ever erected. Lizzie took many photographs of it on her 1890 Grand Tour of Europe--courtesy Howard Davis

Did Lizzie Borden Axe For It?

2. Fiction

Bridget and the Crowe Hatchet

Winter, 1943. Bridget was now an old woman. As sturdy as ever, but now with an even more protruding breast and massive belly. She was ill in bed with pneumonia. She saw that death's dark phantom was coming to claim her life and she wanted to confess something, something she had never told a living soul--a grave secret that was threatening to take itself into the grave with her if she didn't speak soon.

Her husband poured and handed her a cup of camomile tea, holding the cup as he helped her to drink.

"Thank you, dear," she sighed, gasping as she finished her sip.

The sweat glistened from her brow and she seemed half-conscious. She was clinically blind.

"Get me Minnie, please. I must speak to her, if I have any breath left by the time she arrives. I must confess a secret."

Her husband nodded silently, sympathetically, and left the room.

Minnie Green was an old childhood friend; they had known

201

each other well in the old country, Ireland. Bridget had promised Andrew Jennings after the trial that she would go to Ireland and never come back to America. But it was a promise she could not keep, and by 1904, she was back, but careful to move as far away from Fall River as possible, while at the same time being close enough to a good friend: Minnie. Anaconda, Montana seemed the perfect answer. There she met the man who she would one day marry.

Bridget fell asleep for a few hours and then was awakened by the front door closing. She sat up in bed. Suddenly, Bridget was feeling much better. Was it the camomile tea? Was it that she had been resolved to die, therefore no longer fearful of death? Something came over her and she was feeling much better. She was seized by a feeling of gladness.

Her bedroom door opened slowly and a face peeped in. "Oh you poor woman," said Minnie in almost a whisper. "How is the illness?"

Bridget smiled and patted the side of the bed and Minnie hurried over. "Come here, I want you to sit with me."

Minnie, startled to find her in such good spirits, sat down on the bed.

"Your husband tells me that you are going to give me a deathbed confession."

"Nonsense. I've changed my mind. Instead, I'll tell you about Lizzie Borden and the tragedy. You know I've never really spoken about it with you or anyone, and I think it's about time."

"By all means," sighed Minnie. "What would you like to tell me about her?"

"You know, Min, I always liked Lizzie. I understood what she and her sister were displeased about and I secretly took their side, although I sympathized with Mrs. Borden too, as she was a very nice lady. I was so afraid, I was so afraid they would put the murders on me. Why, I couldn't even imagine sitting still in a carriage, I had to walk to the court house to unwind my nerves. The newspapers were cruel to me, hinting that I did it. Partly for fear of my life, I helped Lizzie out. If I had sided with Miss Alice Russell, who knows what Lizzie's lawyers would have said about me! And yet, my conscience is clear. I did not lie on the stand. I could have said more, but as far as a real bold-faced lie . . . I don't recall making one. Maybe only one or two, but they were of little consequence. Lizzie was pleased with me and thanked me personally, even apologizing to me for what I was put through. Oh, and they gave me money for being a defense witness. Mr. Robinson was ever such a nice man, and so was that Andrew Jennings in his way. I got money to go back to Ireland. Enough to buy a farm. I sold it after some ten years or so. Moved to Anaconda, and now many years later here I am in Butte."

Minnie listened closely and as soon as Bridget stopped talking, she spoke out:

"You never told me any of this before."

"I was afraid to. I didn't want anyone to know. It was a promise I made to Mr. Jennings. I didn't want him finding out from the newspapers in those days that I had broken my word. The newspapers in those days were cruel. It hardly matters now, however. Anything I say, it hardly matters now. It's such a long-ago, half-remembered episode in my life. But I've never fully forgotten it, never can. I was a young woman then in my mid-twenties, quite pretty. Now I'm ugly and old . . . and near to dying," she chuckled.

"Oh Bridget," said Minnie, wiping the sweat from her brow with a wet towel, "we all grow gray. Would you like me to leave you now so you can get some sleep?"

"Oh, I'm no longer tired. I'll just do some reading, just leave the light on."

Minnie nodded and started walking away to the door. She then turned around abruptly and said: "I don't know about that

Did Lizzie Borden Axe For It?

Lizzie Borden, but you, you've lived a good and honorable life, without harm to anyone."

Bridget was seized by those last words. Her expression changed from gladness to sadness.

Drawing of Bridget Sullivan, the Borden maid

Did Lizzie Borden Axe For It?

Minnie immediately noticed the shift in mood. "Is anything the matter?" she asked, puzzled.

At first Bridget was silent, but then she spoke in a low tone:

"There is . . . something else, Minnie. I . . . saw something on the morning of the murders."

Minnie hurried back to the bed. "What? What did you see?"

"I had just finished the last windows downstairs and emptied out the bucket. I went upstairs for a nap. It wasn't a terribly hot day, but the air was still and the sun was shining brightly and it felt uncomfortable, stuffy. Anyhow, I felt tired out. I went upstairs to my room for a short nap before 'dinner.' I was sometimes wont to nap for awhile before coming back down to prepare the mid-day meal. I was lying down when I heard the town hall bell striking eleven. It woke me from a daydream and I got up. I looked out my window, I don't know why, and there was Lizzie coming around the back with a . . . with something in her hand. She threw it on the lower roof . . . Mr. Crowe's roof. Just flung it up there as the bell continued to toll. I thought nothing by it, nothing much. Lizzie was known for her eccentricities. Then about ten minutes later, Lizzie hollered up to me. She hollered loud and urgent-like. . . . And that's when I learned that there was murder. It was very frightening. I went to get the doctor, but Mrs. Bowen told me he wasn't home, so I came back and Lizzie fetched me to get Miss Russell, and . . . it was all such a horror. It's a wonder I didn't faint!" Bridget was out of breath and she paused momentarily, grabbing Minnie by the hand and squeezing. "It didn't occur to me until later . . . Lizzie's trip to the backyard. It was a hatchet I saw in her hand, because one was found up there at about the time of the trial. Some carpenter claimed it, but it wasn't his. I don't believe it. I know what I saw. I saw Lizzie . . . and she swung up with her arm . . . and it landed there on that low roof. I know it did. I, I saw it from the window. No one else says they saw but I saw it. There was a high fence and trees everywhere and from where she might have been seen, no one was standing there to see her. . . . Do you believe me, Minnie? Do you believe I saw her?"

"Yes, Bridget. I do."

"I only realized this many hours later when I had calmed down and was in the house with the others . . . and it struck me. I thought perhaps Lizzie had killed them and I wanted to spend the night elsewhere, so I did, with Mr. Miller's maid. Then when I learned the wounds had come from a hatchet and not a knife, I knew sure that Lizzie had done it. But I couldn't say anything, you understand?" she wept, wiping her eyes. "I was afraid they would turn against me and make me the villain. I respected Miss Russell's courage, but I couldn't . . . I couldn't follow her example. I was afraid. I was only a poor and lowly servant, and they could have fed me to the dogs. If Lizzie and her people had turned on me, I couldn't defend myself the way Lizzie could. And Miss Lizzie was so nice to me at any rate, and I, I felt sorry for her . . . I--"

"I understand perfectly," said Minnie, rubbing Bridget's shoulder and hugging her. "No need to say any more, my good woman. You did the best you could. The good Lord will have mercy on you."

Bridget kept weeping guiltily.

Did Lizzie Borden Axe For It?

Lizzie's Boyfriend

David Morse Anthony, Jr. was only 21 years old, but the 32-year-old Lizzie had fallen for him. They had met because he used to deliver meat to the Borden house from his father's wholesale meat business, known as *Anthony & Swift Company*. They took to each other right away. In the beginning they would have pleasant chats in the kitchen, and this quickly evolved into secret night-time trysts by the romantic light of the moon.

Lizzie was fond of telling David how she would have loved to live up in the "Highlands" district of Fall River where the "old money" lived, where the upper crust of Fall River society ruled the roost. The wealthy mill owners, bankers and business-people lived up there in those grand, luxurious mansions and Lizzie wished one day to live there. It was a dream of hers that haunted her every waking hour. It was a dream that could not be reality.

David was a good-looking young man, "tall, dark and handsome" as the saying goes. Lizzie was taken by his clear, bright-blue eyes, attractive red lips, and trim goatee. But it's not only that he was pleasing to look at, she really enjoyed his personality. She felt she could say almost anything to him and feel understood; he had this calm, casual, tolerant air about him that she liked, nothing stiff or narrow-minded. He made her laugh, he made her smile; he was charming.

It was the evening of August 2, 1892. Lizzie met up with him at their secret meeting-place by the broad and brackish Taunton

207

Did Lizzie Borden Axe For It?

River. She saw him already waiting for her with a desperation to hold her. They embraced, kissing in one hard, long, breathless pressure of lips.

David rolled out a blanket so that they could sit down on the slope and look out onto the water. The moon-kissed river was rippling, and the crickets were buzzing.

"I love to fish," said Lizzie, "and as a small girl I bathed in that water."

David nodded silently. He wasn't much given to talk. He and Lizzie were similar in that way.

"I've got to get rid of them," said Lizzie, out of the blue. "Abby and her sister are conspiring against father to trick him . . . to write a will that would leave the bulk of the estate to her and her kin. Well I won't have it! Errgh, it makes me angry! And if you think I'm upset, you should see Emma. But Emma won't stand up to father, she is afraid that it would turn his love cold. Besides, she's a timid, mousy person by nature, whereas I'm not afraid to stand up for myself, for both of us. I've had to at least on one occasion. I tried poisoning them with arsenic, but that didn't work. Maybe I need a better poison? I don't know but that I'll have to kill them as they sleep in their beds!"

David looked at her intensely. "If you could get rid of them, we would be able to be together. We'd be able to marry without your father or that gold-digger Abby standing in our way. Then we'd marry. Then I'd move in to your house--"

Lizzie interrupted him: "wait, I have an idea! . . ."

"What is it?"

She pondered for awhile, her eyes shifting around in deep contemplation. "Do you think you could manage it?"

"Manage what?"

"Kill them."

He paused. "I would do anything for you. I would walk to hell and back."

Did Lizzie Borden Axe For It?

"Do you think you could . . . murder them . . . and get away?"

"Yes."

"And I'll help you. Otherwise you might get caught. . . . I want Abby dead, d-e-a-d, dead. She and her family are a bunch of nobodies, and here they are, trying to go after father's fortune. They'll get nothing!"

"How will we do it?"

"Meet me at the front of the house at exactly 9:00 o'clock, Wednesday night. I'll visit a friend first and say I fear father has an enemy, and so on, so that when the murder occurs people will say it was father's enemy. There are several people from the highest to the lowest in this city who dislike father, for many, many years now. So, I'll meet you by the front gate and smuggle you into the house and into my bedroom. The others will be in bed by that hour, I'm sure. My room is right up the front stairs anyway, whereas they're in the back."

"I'll finish them. Then your father won't be able to stand in our way."

"No, he won't," said Lizzie firmly.

It was a dark night. No stars, no moon. David stood leaning on the post of the gate in front of the house when he saw Lizzie coming from across the street. She crossed and took him by the elbow. The streets were quiet, no one was about. A dog howled in the distance.

Lizzie opened the front door and looked inside. No one in sight. She quickly led David inside and they rushed up the front staircase and into Lizzie's room. Lizzie locked the door behind them and ran into his arms, smothering his whole face with kisses. He collapsed down onto the bed and they made frantic, passionate love.

"You young stud, you make me feel like a school-girl again!" Her tongue probed inside his mouth with a sensual hunger. "Touch my breasts," she said, making him rub the tightly corseted lumps of flesh. He buried his face in her bosom and looked back up at her with an intoxicated, dreamy-eyed glance. "Tomorrow, I have my revenge," said Lizzie, grinning.

Truesdale Hospital; 1926. Lizzie arrived under the assumed name Mary Smith in need of a surgical operation. She was now 66 years old. She had been living comfortably for over three decades but now she was in real discomfort. It was her gallbladder.

Lizzie was put under the care of nurse Ruby Cameron. Ruby liked this sweet, friendly woman, except for her complaints against the hospital food--it wasn't the fine dining she was used to, and she had taken to ordering her meals from fancy restaurants and having them delivered to her in the hospital. But Ruby enjoyed chatting with her patient about "the good old days." She was only 25 years old, herself.

One day after Lizzie's surgery and while she was still recovering, they somehow got on the subject of love. Ruby admitted she had never been in love yet. "What about you?"

Lizzie gave out a deep sigh. "I loved a man once. His name was David Mason Anthony. He wanted to marry me, but our difference in age and social status was a hindrance. My father tried to keep us apart. He couldn't. David loved me too much. He killed to be with me. But then I realized I could never marry him. The murders changed me completely. Everything changed. They all turned on me. People with whom I had been on good terms for years suddenly passed me by on the streets without a word, without so much as a glance. I became the lady of sorrows. I spent my nights and days in nightmarish brooding. I obsessed over what they were thinking of me. It filled me with anxiety and depression. I wanted the whole world to know I wasn't the killer. But although I could no longer love David for what he had done to destroy my reputation, I felt that I could also not turn him in. He died tragically, in an accident 2 years ago. He suffered a skull fracture and he died. I couldn't marry him after what happened. They would have known he was the killer. You know what I mean, don't you?"

"Yes, I think so."

Lizzie momentarily looked emotional, but she shed no tear. She was not the crying kind.

A few days later, Lizzie was back on her feet and leaving the hospital.

"First I must say goodbye to a special friend," she said, and exchanged a warm, heartfelt farewell with Ruby Cameron. "You looked after me very well, thank you."

"Not at all," replied Ruby. "You were a most pleasant patient."

Lizzie was slowly escorted out through the entrance by her chauffeur and into a dark fancy car waiting out in front. Within moments, she was gone.

One of the nurses put her hand around Ruby's waist. "She really seemed to take to you."

"Yes, I suppose so."

"Do you know who she was? We learned not long ago--that was Lizzie Borden."

Ruby's jaw just about dropped down to the floor.

Did Lizzie Borden Axe For It?

Murder Most Horrid

Lizzie went down into the cellar. It was dark. She went into the room where the tool box with hatchets was kept. It was a little before 9 o'clock in the morning. She picked up one hatchet. Too big. She picked up another one. It seemed the right size.

Running back upstairs, she saw that there was no one around. She sneaked over to the front foyer and up the front staircase. The stairs creaked as Lizzie slowly made her way up the steps, eyes wide. When she got to the eleventh step, she looked over and there she was, her stepmother Mrs. Abby Borden, in the guest-room. She had just finished slipping on the new pillow-cases and was tidying up the room for a visit scheduled for the following Monday.

Lizzie hurried up the rest of the steps and stopped at the edge of the doorway to the guest-room. She peeped in. Abby was looking down, smoothing out the bed. Lizzie counted one, two, three in her head and then rushed into the room as fast as she could. She was emboldened by a rage from within. Abby had to be eliminated.

Abby glanced up, astonished, and didn't even have time to move, spotting the hatchet at the last second as it wildly clipped some skin from the side of her head. This spun her around and she fell to her knees. Lizzie struck and struck. Abby's hair-piece was in the way. Lizzie grabbed the "rat" of false hair and threw it on the bed, hacking into the woman's skull with the other hand as quickly as she could. Quick, precise blows that did not miss their mark.

212

Did Lizzie Borden Axe For It?

Abby groaned as she fell face-first onto the floor. Lizzie got astride her, and bending down, delivered a few more blows just for good measure.

"You bitch, you bitch . . ." Lizzie murmured in her hoarse, mannish voice. Her face was beet-red and her mouth was contorted in anger.

She stopped swinging. Suddenly, all was still again. She looked at the blade, dripping with fresh blood. Lizzie realized that she would have to wipe the blade first if she was going to take it anywhere, otherwise it would drip all over the place, so she put the hatchet down momentarily and ran downstairs. Lizzie got a piece of handkerchief from the dining-room, took it back upstairs, and smeared the blood of the hatchet into it. With the blade now relatively dry, she went downstairs again and into the sitting-room. There she rested the hatchet against the fireplace where it wouldn't be particularly noticed or out of place.

Within minutes, she was in the dining-room ironing some of her favorite handkerchiefs. But on purpose she wasn't doing a good job of getting the flats hot, and while she waited for her father to come home, she sat down to read the *Harper's Weekly*. There was no shock over just having bashed her step-mother's brains in. She thought about it now very calmly and rationally, with a detachment one sees only in the most disturbed individuals completely unhindered by conscience.

At 10:40 AM, Andrew came back to the house from his daily rounds and tried to get in through the side door. Locked. He knocked. No one opened. Andrew marched to the front door and tried his key, but the door was bolted. He knocked.

Bridget, the maid, was inside wiping the windows. She hurried to the front door. "Pshaw!" she sighed in frustration as she was having trouble with the lock.

Lizzie, who was standing on the stairs watching her, laughed aloud.

Did Lizzie Borden Axe For It?

Finally the door opened and Andrew walked in, tired, worn-out, with sweat on his face. He was looking a bit under the weather.

Lizzie came down and over to him. "Any mail?"

"None for you," he replied.

Andrew took a seat down in the dining-room. He needed a moment to rest. There was a white package in his hands and he laid it on the table.

Getting up awhile later, he took the package up the back stairs into his bedroom with him and changed into a sweater. It was a sunny, humid day, but not really hot. Andrew came into the sitting-room and sat down in a rocking-chair by one of the windows. The curtains were open and he looked out into the somewhat busy street bustling with carriages and pedestrians.

Lizzie waited as Bridget finished putting away her pail and brush for washing windows. She watched her as she went up the backstairs to her attic room.

Lizzie came inside the sitting-room. "Are you feeling better now father? Not ill anymore?"

Andrew laughed. "I suppose I'm all right now. Feeling just a little off. Not too bad."

"Here, let me help you get comfortable on the sofa."

Andrew got up and staggered over to it, sitting back cozily. Lizzie puffed his cushion for him and he leaned back against it.

"Thank you, Lizzie."

"You are most welcome, father." Lizzie gave him one of those smiles which he had rarely seen in the last dozen years or so. She smiled at him as she used to in her teens, when she had loved him so, when they were allies, when he was on her side and a gold ring she had given him symbolized their allegiance.

She pranced over to the windows. "I'll just close these curtains so that the light doesn't bother your eyes."

He nodded indifferently, still sitting up, with eyes closed and head leaning back. He had laid down his newspaper.

214

Did Lizzie Borden Axe For It?

Lizzie watched him for a few moments. He seemed to be dozing off to sleep. She inched over to the fireplace and bent down, grabbing the handle of the hatchet tightly. Her heart felt like it was beating inside her ears--boom, boom, boom! In an abrupt burst, she scurried over towards her father, who just as abruptly opened his eyes and turned his head, only to see the sharp edge swinging down on him. Whack! his eyeball cut in two, leaks out from his face; whack! his jaw is dislodged. He groans as Abby had groaned, but more feebly. Lizzie slices his nose and crushes into the side of his face some more. He slumps over, exposing the entire left side of his head. Lizzie re-adjusts her position and delivers the heaviest blows, crushing the side of the head open. A huge skull piece is stuck down right against the brains. Blood is everywhere. But Lizzie, like before, has only been very lightly sprinkled, hardly enough to leave any obvious trace. The blood splattered away from her. The bloody hatchet dripped again as it had dripped with Abby, except this time even more. The skull damage was even more severe with her father.

Lizzie quickly wiped the blade into Andrew's Prince Albert coat and ran into the cellar with the blade. She broke off the handle, pumped plenty of water over the blade to rinse out any other spec of blood, and still wet, dipped the blade into coal ash to make it look like an old and unused blade which could not have been the murder weapon. But the cut of the handle was fresh. She left the handle and blade in a tool box.

It was all catching up with her now, the fatigue, and Lizzie felt like fainting. But her stubborn resolve gave her new energy and strength. Gasping as she ran, she sprinted up to the first floor and over to the backstairs, crying aloud:

"Maggie, come down quick! Somebody came in and stabbed father!"

3. Humor

Lizzie's New Hat

My impression of Lizzie inviting a relative over for a private late-night candle-light dinner.

Knock, knock. Terence comes to the door. It's Nellie Miller, Lizzie's maid. She hands him a card. Terence looks at it, flips it over. Its an invite. Lizzie has invited her close acquaintance and relative, Terence Borden, over for some roast duck. An appropriate high-class meal. At first, Terence hesitates, but then he nods to the maid and tells her he'll be honored to accept the invitation. The polite but embarrassed grin on his face betrays his real reservations about it. Lizzie has some friends but she's always been an intensely private woman. Even as a young girl she was reclusive and not quick to make friends. She's feeling especially lonely and would like to share a succulent meal with her favorite cousin and one of her kindest, starchest--I mean, *staunchest*, defenders.

Terence dresses up in his best suit and necktie. He dons a big top-hat and looks quite the dandy dandy. It's a pleasant night out. Terence hails a cab (the horse 'n' buggy kind) and gives the

216

driver the address. The cabbie gives him a strange look but shakes the reins and the galloping begins.

Terence arrives at 7 in the evening, exactly on time as if it were the work of divine providence. He's admitted into the house and asked to wait at the entrance while the maid goes to summon cousin Lizzie. Lizzie comes down the stairs; she is dressed in a very sleek black silk dress and her hair is in pigtails--no, her hair is in a stylish bun. She looks quite . . . ordinary--no, no, Lizzie looks ravishing in her fancy silk, her cheeks rouged and eye-liner bringing out her eyes. Actress Nance O'Neil had taught her to use make-up. Her piercing eyes are hypnotic and her plump sensual lips look made to bite--or kiss, or suck.

"Come into the dining-room," she says to Terence.

They take their seats across from each other at the fine mahogany table. Terence looks around. The room is dim except for the candles burning. He feels noticeably uneasy. Reaches for his glass to wet his dry throat. But he reaches too nervously, too fast and accidentally knocks the red wine over. "Oh God, I feel such a fool!"

"Not at all, dear Terry, I'll get Nellie to wipe it."

Lizzie smiles at Terence and stares at him dreamily for a few moments without even appearing to notice. This makes Terence feel even more nervous and disconcerted.

"S-so," he stammers, "what's life like in this place?"

"Well, ever since Emma left last year, it's a lot quieter, more lonely. I travel less and less these days and . . . "

The maid brings the duck. Mmm! This wets Terence's gums and he momentarily forgets about his apprehensions. No grace, they just dig in. What delicious juicy meat! At the end, they wipe their mouths and lean back in their seats. Terence adjusts his belt buckle because he feels very full, but Lizzie licks her lips and gets other ideas from it.

"I'd like to show you something," says Lizzie.

217

Did Lizzie Borden Axe For It?

"What?" asks Terence, gulp.

"My new hat-choo," she sneezes.

"Your what?"

"My hat--"

"Your new hatchet?!" Terence sighs aloud, fainting on the spot in fear.

"No, silly, my new *hat*," she laughs.

But Terence is passed out on the floor, unconscious.

Did Lizzie Borden Axe For It?

My Impression of the Lizzie Borden Trial

The giant, bull-like frame of Hosea Knowlton dominating the floor like a freak of nature, a colossus of flesh; the lean, attractive, clean-cut, well-spoken William H. Moody being ogled by all the many ladies in attendance fluttering their eye-lashes at him and giving him flirty looks and smiles as he gives a fine opening argument for the prosecution; George Dexter Robinson skilfully examining and cross-examining witnesses, trying to get anything which even hints at Lizzie's guilt excluded by objecting to this line of questioning or that, no matter how relevant the question happens to be; the short, mannish, butchy figure of Lizzie sitting there in "the dock", sniffing her "smelling bottle" like an ether addict while Pastor Judd fans her with her fan in an attempt to keep her conscious in the stifling heat of the room. Lizzie wears a fashionable black mohair dress with leg-of-mutton sleeves. She pays very close attention during the testimony of certain witnesses, like her sister Emma, and once or twice she's brought to fainting or tears, especially when the Prosecution brings the victims' skulls into the court room; she walks out and prefers to wait in the hall. Lizzie laughs out loud when Bridget makes eye contact with her and testifies about the stale mutton soup they had been eating four breakfasts in a row on the morning of the murders. But most of the time Lizzie just sits there very still and unemotional, dreaming of her life after the trial. She's aware that all points in her favor, especially since the exclusion of that pesky, self-incriminating inquest testimony, and she knows that

219

Did Lizzie Borden Axe For It?

freedom lurks just on the horizon if she can just bear it all a little bit longer and not give in one inch. "It'll be alright, little girl," says her lawyer Robinson, comfortingly patting her shoulder. Her mind is full of romance as she sits there, half-conscious, half-comprehending all that proceeds around her. Little does she know that one day a young, good-looking French chauffeur will sweep her off her feet-- not that ugly sentimental doltish Curtis Pierce with his childish schoolboy fantasies and inept attempts at lovemaking. Lizzie wants a real and experienced lover, and one who won't hound her obsessively and embarrass and annoy her. Suddenly, she snaps out of her daydream to the sound of the gavel's bang and Judge Blodgett adjourning the jury for 9 o'clock the next morning.

A sketch of Lizzie in court. Of all the many courtroom drawings of Lizzie that were done by various newspaper artists, this is perhaps the only accurate likeness of her

Hosea Merrill Knowlton

*A rare photo of the lead prosecutor in the trial of Lizzie Borden,
Hosea Knowlton, when he was a young man studying law--from
the Tufts College Yearbook 1867, courtesy Faye Musselman*

Did Lizzie Borden Axe For It?

Work consulted:
Joyce G. Williams, Eric Smithburn and M. Jeanne Peterson, *Lizzie Borden: A Casebook of Family and Crime in the 1890's*

Lizzie cartoon--courtesy Rick London

Did Lizzie Borden Axe For It?

Lizzie killer doll--source unknown

Did Lizzie Borden Axe For It?

Let me introduce you to my favorite little game called "Lizzie Borden"!--private collection

Did Lizzie Borden Axe For It?

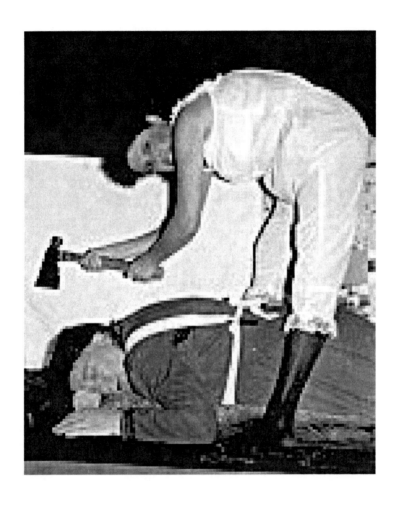

I won't say good morning, but good night, Abby!--private collection

Did Lizzie Borden Axe For It?

Hey, who says that fans of Lizzie are kooks and crazies!--private collection

Did Lizzie Borden Axe For It?

My Impression of Visiting Lizzie at Maplecroft

I would've been one of those thrill-seekers who paid the cab-driver to take him to the house of Massachusetts' most infamous murderess. He'd stop in front of the house. I'd have taken my spiffy straw hat off and popped my head out of the motor-car window as far as I could, looking on wide-eyed and aghast. The cabby, quite used to people's morbid and sensationalistic curiosity about Lizzie, would wax eloquent about the woman, her trial, etc, peppering his dialogue with more than its fair share of embellishments and made-up bits to thrill my ears. Then, after he had started repeating himself and was running out of new material, I'd say cheerio and get out of the car and make my way cautiously, fearfully up to the house. I'd feel like a little kid walking up to a haunted house all alone. Knock, knock, knock. Three sharp knocks. Lizzie's maid opens.

"Hi, I'd like to see Miss Lizzie Borden."

The maid frowns. "Miss *Lizbeth* is at Swansea at the moment. What are you here for? I'll tell her you stopped by."

Suddenly, a car parks out at the side of the street. Chauffeur Ernest Terry gets out and opens the passenger door. And there she is, the woman herself. Somewhat plump, a face without expression, walking in a stiff and haughty gait. I'm standing there speechless on the marble steps.

The chauffeur notices me and runs up, asking none too kindly: "what's your business here? What d'you want?"

"I'd just like to speak with Miss–"

Did Lizzie Borden Axe For It?

"Well Miss Liz don't allow no visitors. If you ain't her lawyer, you ain't welcome. She only accepts friends and acquaintances and people that got to do with her business affairs and such. I ain't ever seen you b'fore."

"I'm . . . new to the area."

"Well I can already tell you's one o' dem reeeeporters or journalists come to do a bit o' snoopin' huh? Well, git! Leave da little lady alone now would ya?!"

The plump, wobbling, gray-haired, solemn-eyed matron would make her way into the house and I would make like I was leaving. Then as soon as they were in the house, I'd run around to the side and back yard. I'd try to get in through a downstairs window, that's what I'd do! Oh damn, there's bars over the windows to keep out nosy weirdos like me! Oops, a dog starts barking. I better get outta here before this growling mutt takes a bite outta my ass and makes a meal of it! I'd leave satisfied and thrilled. How many others would be able to say they'd gotten that close to the woman, to the house?

Did Lizzie Borden Axe For It?

A fake Lizzie photo. There is no known photo of Lizzie Borden in her late years.

Did Lizzie Borden Axe For It?

This Lizzie photo appeared in the previous edition of this book but has since been identified as a fake--from Dan Dunn Collectibles

Did Lizzie Borden Axe For It?

My Impression of Meeting Lizzie at the Theatre

Scene: the theatre lobby; an intermission between acts.

DAVE: Miss Borden, I am pleased to make your acquaintance. I followed your trial with much interest in the *Fall River Daily Globe*, your case aroused much sympathy in me for your sufferings. Such a long and unwarranted 10-month detention behind bars--it's a scandal! How terrible that you were even suspected of such a crime simply because the incompetent police couldn't find the culprit, so they were covering their own incompetency by accusing the only person they rightly could--you. . . . But I must say, you seem to have recovered remarkably well from the entire ordeal, and you're lookin' awfully chipper.

MISS BORDEN (blushes): Thank you, Mr . . .

DAVE: Rehak. I'm from a land far away. I was born in a town in eastern Moravia called Zlin. The word "zli" means "bad" and when you add the "n" at the end of the word, it means "place or home of bad people" in my native tongue. It appears that when the town was first established back in the 16th century, it was a place well-known for drunkenness, debauchery, theft, and murder.

MISS BORDEN: You don't say. . .

DAVE: Oh, I do, ma'am. Hey, speaking of murder, you didn't happen to, oh, I don't know . . . bludgeon those pesky old parents of yours, did you? Not that I believe it myself, just asking.

MISS BORDEN: I beg your pardon! (Tears fill her eyes.) Like I said, I said I know nothing about it--nothing!

DAVE: Ya, ya, ya. And camels fly. Hey lady, do you really think St. Peter's gonna let you through when you come knockin' on Heaven's gate?

MISS BORDEN: I'm sure I don't know what you mean, but if you are implying what I think you are, I do believe myself worthy of every heavenly reward, both in this life and the next, as a good and innocent woman, thank you very much!

DAVE: Hey lady, in the final scene of the final act, Hedda Gabler is gonna blow her brains out. Have you seen it?--not the scene in the play, but someone's brains, I mean?

MISS BORDEN: Certainly not!

DAVE: But you saw your father on the couch. You said so.

MISS BORDEN: Well, yes, but all I saw was blood.

DAVE: What happened to the hatchet?

MISS BORDEN (very nervous): How am I to know?! I was in the "bahn."

LIZZIE'S COACHMAN (stepping forward and brushing me aside): I demand that you stop tormenting this poor lady with your accusatory language! She was found "*not* guilty", yes, *not guilty*, have you no ears? Have you no sense of what is right and proper? Off with you, be off! Brute! You should be locked up!

Did Lizzie Borden Axe For It?

4. Poetry

Lizzie Borden, Shame on You!

Lizzie Borden, shame on you!
Chopped the old folks' heads in two
You can't fix that up with glue!
Lizzie Borden

That Yellow-Haired Sun, . . .

That yellow-haired Sun,
Great Father of the Azure,
Beat down like a drum
With His tantalizing lure
Of warmth and gladness.

But on 92 Second Street,
Oppressive was the heat!
And not a drop to cool the anger,
Not a smile to still the rancour.

232

Did Lizzie Borden Axe For It?

First the one, then the other;
Such a mess made of father & mother.
But their souls climb the celestial steps,
As their bodies lie in their earthen rest.

Lizzie Borden, Fess Up Now . . .

Lizzie Borden, fess up now
Did you level that old sow?
And when father went to lay
Did you make that old scrooge pay?

Lizzie Borden, tell me straight
Was there really that much hate?
Was he gonna change the will?
Is that why you had to kill?

Lizzie Borden, please don't lie
So much pretense! don't even try!
Did they really have to die?
Why'd ya do it, why oh why.

233

Did Lizzie Borden Axe For It?

Lizzie Borden Nursery Rhyme

Come little Lizzie, don't you cry
Daddy's gonna give you his favorite axe
And if that old axe don't kill,
Daddy's gonna buy you one that will!

But you better not use it on your stepmum now
She may be bovine--yes, shaped like a cow
But I love her more than you, it's true
She knows how to treat me, unlike you two!

So here's the axe, a gift from me
Make sure you put it to good use
My money went to pay for it, y'know
Sharp enough to cut down any tree or foe

But you love me, this I know
I'll always be wearing that ring
On my finger where'er I go
Even at the axe's first swing!

234

Did Lizzie Borden Axe For It?

Blame It On The Beau

Lizzie Borden said she had a beau
But we know she was lying tho
'Cos she's the one who swung the axe
And no amount of lying can change the facts.

She says this boyfriend did the act.
The end result--two people got hacked.
But I don't buy your story Liz.
At the game of lying you're such a wiz.

And if I had a penny for your every lie,
Stinking rich I'd live and die.
And if I ever heard you tell the truth,
It'd be by mistake or my name's Doctor Ruth!

A Mad Lizzie

Lizzie Borden got real mad
Couldn't stand her cheap-o dad
Swingin' that hatchet made her glad
Got her half-a-mil' and that ain't half bad!

Did Lizzie Borden Axe For It?

Lizzie To Emma:

A friend in greed
Is a friend indeed!
And you're my own sister,
Which is even better.

We got away with it, ain't it grand!
Got those stupid jurors eating right out of my
hand!

We got away with it, ain't it grand!
But you know I had to, I had to take a stand.
Couldn't let Abby keep him round her little finger.
You know I was most justified to commit murder!
O but look how to the better my life has changed
And to hell if some call me evil or deranged!

Did Lizzie Borden Axe For It?

Lizzie's Axe

Lizzie where'd you put that axe?
God you're cunning as a fox!

Lizzie, y'ain't so bright but you're clever
as hell.
How'd ya get away with those lies
so well?

Was it in the barn or bedroom, basement or roof?
The day will never come when we'll have the proof.
But in this search to claim the truth,
Each of us is a tireless armchair sleuth!

V. Appendices

Public Reaction to the Trial Verdict

PROVIDENCE JOURNAL
Wednesday, June 21, 1893
The Verdict

With the proceedings at New Bedford yesterday one of the most celebrated criminal trials of modern times comes to an end. Lizzie Borden has been adjudged not guilty by a jury of her peers, after a careful presentation of evidence, elaborate arguments by distinguished counsel and a lucid charge by a learned judge [note: Judge Dewey's charge is commonly held to have been biased in Lizzie's favor]. There is no doubt of the fairness of the trial, so far as the prisoner is concerned, or of the honesty of the jury in reaching a verdict upon the facts laid before them. But it would be idle to assert that this outcome of the case is satisfactory. Those who believe Miss Borden to be guilty will hardly be swayed by it, and those who believe her to be innocent will regret that some positive proof was not adduced. No more brutal murders were ever committed, and that the murderer should escape is revolting to the public sense of justice. Now that Miss Borden is free she should lose no time and spare no effort in trying to secure the detection of the real criminal. She owes this much to the memory of her dead father and stepmother, and to her own reputation. Others than the jury are not bound by the ruling of the Court, and they cannot help giving weight to that portion of the Government's case which was not admitted but which could not fail in some degree to compromise her.

There has been throughout the trial a disposition in many quarters to criticise with undo severity the conduct of the District Attorney [prosecutor Hosea Knowlton] and his associates. But surely no fair-minded person, bearing in mind Miss Borden's own statements, to say nothing of all the circumstances of the crime, can deny that there was ample reason for the arrest and prosecution. Nor is it just to say that their theory as to Miss Borden's guilt made them indisposed to follow up other possible subjects of suspicion. On the contrary, the most unpromising clues were diligently followed. That Mr. Knowlton himself believed firmly in the strength of his case, that he reached the conclusions he set forth so eloquently with deep reluctance and with a full sense of his responsibility, there is no reason to doubt. His closing argument was a masterly presentation of that side of the case, and we regret to say that it has carried conviction to many minds, in spite of the verdict. Such an outcome is inevitable in a case so strange, so unparalleled as this. No one has any desire to see Miss Borden proved guilty; every one instinctively shrinks from a conclusion so horrible. But there is no use in shutting our eyes to the fact that she leaves the courtroom at New Bedford still under a grave cloud of suspicion.

Arguments about the monstrosity of the crime, of the absurdity of imputing it to the daughter of the murdered man, are of little value. The workings of the human heart, like the decrees of fate, are inscrutable. Men and women of apparently blameless lives have many times in the history of the world become all of a sudden little less than fiends. It is not so very long since a respectable woman, the last person in the world whom her friends and neighbors would have suspected of such an act, poisoned her children in cold blood for the sake of the money which the insurance on their lives would bring. And it is not inconceivable, however revolting the thought may be, that one situated as Miss Borden was, surrounded

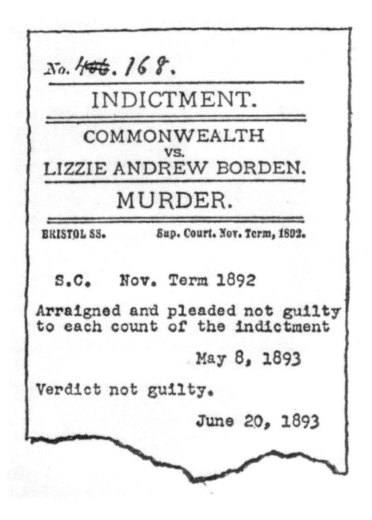

Indictment of Lizzie Borden

Did Lizzie Borden Axe For It?

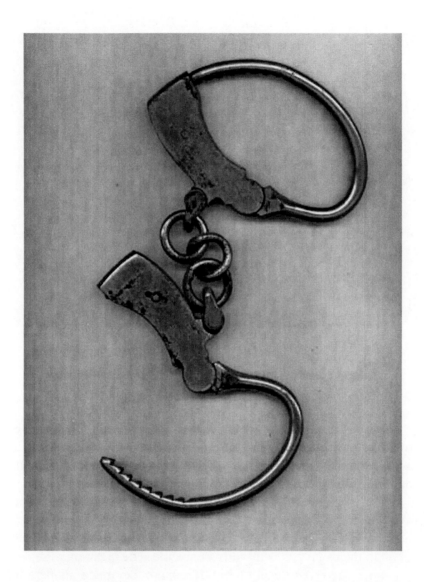

These handcuffs from the late 19th c. were used by the Fall River police (possibly on Lizzie Borden) and were found in the attic of what is today the North End Fire Station on North Main Street, Fall River--private collection

Did Lizzie Borden Axe For It?

Bristol County Courthouse where Lizzie went on trial

by a sordid atmosphere which choked out natural affection and stifled innocent tastes, living after a glimpse of the outer world in the narrow and squalid circle of petty avarice, dowered with the sour and self-concentrated Puritan temperament, should be wrought to a pitch of unnatural frenzy and endeavor to free herself by a deed from which the most hardened criminal might shrink. Moral wracks enough have been wrought elsewhere by the same conditions, although the usual end is insanity or suicide. The question of motive may be barred out legally, but it cannot be made inoperative ethically. Then take all the circumstances of the murder. Did Miss Borden have "exclusive opportunity," as the Government sought to

Did Lizzie Borden Axe For It?

prove? Perhaps not, and yet it is difficult to see how two such murders could have been committed without her knowledge. It is to be said in her behalf that the assumption of her guilt presupposes an iron will, great cunning, and the most favorable conditions. How far all these things existed every one who has followed the case can judge for himself. It is certainly quite as extraordinary to suppose that any person from outside the house could have gained access undetected at such a time, murdered Mrs. Borden, waited more than an hour for the return of Mr. Borden, murdered him, and then escaped leaving absolutely no trace. Yet that is what the verdict compels us to suppose. Mr. Borden, to be sure, was not an agreeable man, and he undoubtedly had many enemies. But who had any motive for killing Mrs. Borden? Or is there any reason to believe, from the position of her body, from the absence of any outcry, which must surely have been heard by Miss Borden, who was in the house at the time, that it was detection or fear of interruption by her which led to this first brutal butchery? And why should the outer door have been bolted and locked by one whose only anxiety was to get away from the house unharmed? We have no desire to press the points, to interpret their meaning one way or the other, to question the justice of the legal acquittal of the prisoner. But so long as they remain unsolved, so long will people be found to place the same interpretation upon them which Mr. Knowlton placed.

The inaccuracies and inconsistencies of Miss Borden's testimony at the preliminary hearing [inquest], concerning which the jury were not called upon to decide, stand in imminent need of explanation, and Miss Borden owes it to her friends, no less than to herself, to endeavor to explain them. The story about the note which Mrs. Borden received from "a sick friend," who has been strangely silent during all these proceedings, the visit to the barn [at around 11 o'clock AM], the allusions to Mrs. Borden after the [Andrew Borden] murder had been discovered, the burning of the dress, the [Wednesday evening] conversation with Miss Russell--upon all

Did Lizzie Borden Axe For It?

these points some clearer light should be thrown. There is no reason now for Miss Borden's silence; let her speak. And let her also, as we have said, spare no effort to bring this horrible case to a more satisfactory conclusion than it has now reached after months of investigation by the Government and floods of eloquence from the defence, with so much evidence barred out by the Court and the presumption of innocence most strenuously insisted upon by the learned judge who delivered the charge.

This *Providence Journal* article above is an excellent indication of the thoughts and sentiments that were going through people's minds and flying off their lips immediately following the verdict. There were the people who believed Lizzie guilty and were displeased; then there were those who thought her innocent and were happy for her release; and lastly, there were those who expressed the opinion of this article--that being, they believed that Lizzie could not be found guilty based on the evidence that was allowed in court, but that it was possible that she committed the murders, and either way, the verdict left a bad taste in their mouths because the "real killer" was presumably still out there, and many questions about Lizzie's supposed innocence still remained unanswered.

A drawing of the three judges that presided over the trial of Lizzie Borden

Did Lizzie Borden Axe For It?

Lizzie Borden's Will

Lizzie's Last Will & Testament was made out, signed and filed in 1926 at the official records in the Second District Court of Fall River. It was the year before she passed away, just a few years before the Great Depression began. At the time of her death, her fortune was estimated to be worth almost 300, 000 dollars, which in today's money is almost 10 million. Lizzie lived a withdrawn and reclusive life much of the time, with her driver and maids. She owned quite a bit of exquisite jewellery including diamond and sapphire rings; many financial investments in stocks; two big cars including a Buick sedan; and several expensive properties including the prominent A. J. Borden Building in Fall River's downtown. Her house was large and comfortable but built in a plain old style and not especially grand or fancy. It was situated on the corner of French and Belmont Streets. In her Will, Lizzie distributed her wealth mostly among her old schoolmates including Addie Whipp and Lucy Macomber; servants such as Ernest Terry and Nellie Miller; and the relatives and friends who were close to her in the post-acquittal years, like Helen Leighton and Grace Howe. Lizzie also willed a considerable sum to the city of Fall River for the perpetual care of her father's grave. Especially interesting, and no doubt surprising to her contemporaries, was her bequest of 30, 000 dollars and her lucrative share of stock in the Stevens Manufacturing Company to the Fall River Animal Rescue League, which was one-seventh of her entire estate. Lizzie was keenly aware of the plight of

Did Lizzie Borden Axe For It?

abused and unwanted animals in a time when there was less respect for animal life and rights.

Work consulted:
Fall River Police Department, Lizzie's Last Will and Testament

Charles Cook, Lizzie's financial advisor and executor of her estate--private collection

Did Lizzie Borden Axe For It?

My Ain Countrie

Mary August Lee Demarest

I am far from home, and I'm weary after while
for the longing for home and my Father's welcome smile.
And I'll never be full content, until my eyes do see,
the golden gates of heaven and my ain countrie

The earth is flecked with flowers tinted fresh and gay,
the birds sing brightly for my Father made them say.
But these sights and these sounds will as nothing be to me,
when I hear the angels singing in my ain countrie.

. . . .

My sins have been many, and my sorrow has been sore,
but this they'll never vex me, nor be remembered more.
For His blood has made me white and His hand shall dry my eye,
When he brings me home at last to my ain countrie

. . . .

Like a child to its mother, a little bird to its nest,
I would want to be going now, unto my Saviour's breast.
For He gathers in His bosom, witless, worthless lambs like me,
and carries them Himself, to his ain countrie

Did Lizzie Borden Axe For It?

The words to this poem are inscribed on the mantel at Maplecroft and the italics are my own. Is it Lizzie's confession from beyond the grave? The first stanza can be interpreted to mean that she misses her father. The second stanza reminds one of Lizzie's love of birds and other animals. The third stanza is most telling about her religious attitude to the murders if she was the murderer. The last stanza suggests that she wants to be forgiven by God (even for the murder, if she did it) and go to Heaven. Indeed, if she sees herself in this poem as a "lamb", in the last stanza Lizzie pictures herself as going to "his ain countrie", meaning God's Heaven.

It is well-documented that Lizzie was a very religious Christian in her own way throughout her adult life. Although she was shunned at church after the acquittal, she continued to read and study the Bible and to live out its benevolent teachings. Many of her charitable acts have been recounted and re-told, but some remain unknown to this day, as people close to Lizzie stated after her death that Lizzie often preferred to carry out these deeds in secret or anonymously through somebody else. Perhaps she was inspired in this by a certain passage of scripture in the Book of Matthew, 6:1-5. If Lizzie was innocent of the murders, then these good deeds were simply a heartfelt expression of her good side. However, if she was the murderer, then these acts had another dimension to them, something of deeper significance: they were partly the result of a guilty conscience, they were her self-imposed penance for breaking the most important of the Ten Commandments, "thou shalt not kill." Christian theology teaches that God will forgive any and every sin, even murder, if it is followed by sincere and earnest repentance. No doubt a guilty Lizzie would offer up her prayer of repentance to God in private, just as she made various acts of generosity in secret. But is "secret repentance" real repentance, or should a guilty Lizzie have repented publicly with an open confession to the murders? But again, she might be partly or completely innocent to begin with.

Did Lizzie Borden Axe For It?

An Obituary of Lizzie Borden

"Miss Lizbeth A. Borden died this morning at 306 French Street, where she had made her home for about 30 years. She had been ill with pneumonia for about a week, although for some time she had been in failing health.

"A member of one of the old Fall River families, having been the daughter of Andrew J. and Sarah (Anthony) Borden, she had lived here all her life. With her two maids she lived a quiet, retired life, paying occasional visits to out-of-town friends and receiving a few callers, whose staunch friendship she valued highly.

"Taking an intense pride in the surroundings in which she lived, she did much to improve the locality, purchasing adjoining property that the same refined atmosphere might be maintained. Greatly interested in nature, she was daily seen providing for the hundreds of birds that frequented the trees in her yard, taking care that the shallow box where they gathered was filled with crumbs, seeds and other foods that they favored. She had miniature houses erected in her trees, and in these, frivolous squirrels made their homes . . .

"Another pastime in which she greatly delighted was riding through the country roads and lanes. She made frequent trips about the town in her [carriage, and later her] motor car but was never so pleased as when winding through the shady country by-ways.

Surviving Miss Borden is a sister, Miss Emma Borden of New Hampshire, formerly of Providence" (Lizbeth Borden Dies

Did Lizzie Borden Axe For It?

After Short Illness, Age 68, *The Fall River Daily Globe*, June 2, 1927).

Lizzie Borden's grave--courtesy Faye Musselman

Did Lizzie Borden Axe For It?

Recommended Reading/Viewing

FUN READS. For the casual Lizzie Borden reader, here are some suggestions:

1.   Victoria Lincoln, *A Private Disgrace: Lizzie Borden By Daylight*. This account is sometimes based on conjecture and has its errors; also sources are usually not cited. However, it's extremely informative, quite plausible, and possibly the most entertaining Lizzie book in the non-fiction category. It won the Best Fact Crime Book award in 1967.

2.   Elizabeth Engstrom, *Lizzie Borden*. Perhaps the most well-written Lizzie novel. Lizzie is sympathetically portrayed. She has a lesbian affair with Bridget, the maid.

3.   Evan Hunter, *Lizzie*. Lizzie goes abroad to Europe and has a lesbian affair with a wealthy and amoral Englishwoman.

4.   William L. Masterton, *Lizzie Didn't Do It!* A very readable non-fiction Lizzie book. The first two-thirds where Masterton deals mostly with just the facts (though somewhat selectively) are the strongest part of the book. The last third where he theorizes is less effective. He's perhaps not a very convincing theorist, but he does write well and this book is a really fun read, with a few humorous

witticisms thrown in.

5.   Frank Spiering, *Lizzie.* A well-written account of the Borden case that nevertheless plays fast and loose with the facts. Written almost in a novelistic style. Indeed, there are times when one forgets he is reading what is supposed to be non-fiction. The author theorizes that Emma killed the elder Bordens.

6. Rick Geary, *The Borden Tragedy: A Memoir of the Infamous Double Murder at Fall River, Mass., 1892.* A short but entertaining comic book rendition of the Borden saga. The story is told in black-and-white drawings which will be especially appreciated by those who like their story told in pictures.

ESSENTIAL READS. For the serious Lizzie Borden reader who wants just the facts of the case and to get down to the nagging truth(s) of it all:

1.   *The Superior Court Trial Transcript of the Lizzie Borden Murder Case, June 5 - 20, 1893.* The most important article of the Lizzie Borden murder mystery.

2.   *The Witness Statements for the Lizzie Borden Murder Case, August 4 - October 6, 1892.* Statements recorded by Fall River police officers of people connected to the tragedy for about a month following the murders.

3.   Leonard Rebello, *Lizzie Borden, Past & Present: A*

Did Lizzie Borden Axe For It?

Comprehensive Reference to the Life and Times of Lizzie Borden. Presented in bibliographical style, the longest and arguably the most complete and comprehensive Lizzie book written to date.

4. Edmund L. Pearson, *Trial of Lizzie Borden.* Pearson's 1937 book and other writings on Lizzie are credited with reviving a strong interest in the Borden case, and all writers on the case who followed owe him a debt of gratitude for that.

5. David Kent, *The Lizzie Sourcebook.* A plethora of newspaper articles written following the murders, at the time of the trial, and after.

6. Robert Sullivan, *Goodbye Lizzie Borden.* An analysis of the Borden case from a legal point of view.

FILM / TV DOCUMENTARIES. For those who also wish to study or explore the Borden murder case visually, here is a list of the videos:

1. Case Reopened: Lizzie Borden with Ed McBain (1999).

2. History's Mysteries--Strange Case of Lizzie Borden (2001).

3. Biography--Lizzie Borden: A Woman Accused (1995).

4. The Legend of Lizzie Borden (1975).

5. Lizzie Borden Hash & Rehash (1996).

6. Lizzie Borden: A Hundred Years of Fascination (1993).

Did Lizzie Borden Axe For It?

NOTE: Lizzie playwright / researcher Eric Stedman, who once put out an audio CD of Lizzie Borden's inquest testimony, is also currently working on a Lizzie Borden documentary in DVD format.

Did Lizzie Borden Axe For It?

Ground Plan of the Borden Residence

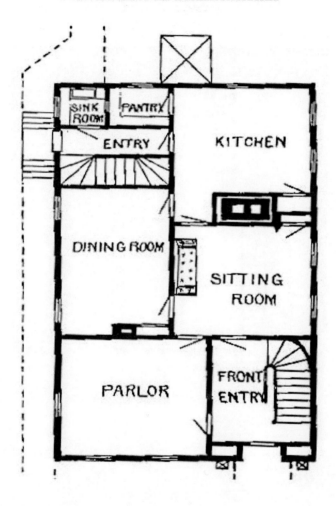

Ground floor of Borden house--from Edwin H. Porter, The Fall River Tragedy

255

Did Lizzie Borden Axe For It?

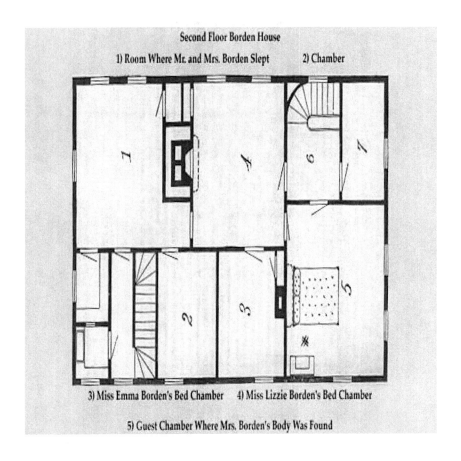

Second floor of Borden house--from Edwin H. Porter, *The Fall River Tragedy*

Did Lizzie Borden Axe For It?

Second Street, 1877. The Borden house may be the one with the question mark, or the one with the three X's. See if you can tell which--from TheHistoryCD.com Vintage Panoramic Maps Collection

Did Lizzie Borden Axe For It?

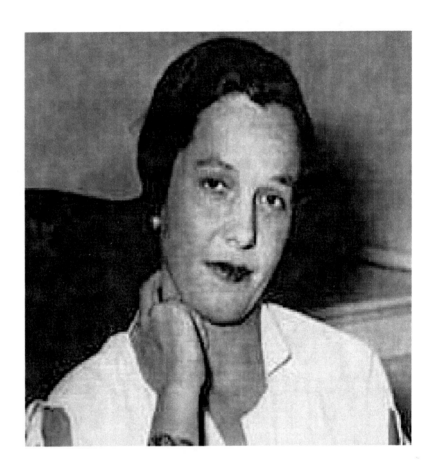

Cornelia Otis Skinner, a Fall River native who was a famous actress and author. She alleged that Lizzie stole a woman's underwear. It is uncertain whether this story is true or just a figment of someone's lewd imagination--from findagrave.com

Did Lizzie Borden Axe For It?

STARVING IN THE MIDST OF PLENTY.

An old erotic postcard from Boston at the turn-of-the-19th-century depicting two women kissing while a gentleman looks on. The humorous caption reads: "Starving in the midst of plenty"

Did Lizzie Borden Axe For It?

Afterword

If anyone wonders why I seem to have such a great deal of sympathy for the victims of this case and a drive to try and solve these murders, I'll tell you. I know what it feels like to have a loved one who was mutilated--even his legs chopped off--and to have the coroner file the death away as "unexplained." I understand the profound pain and grief that is wrought by the hands of a murderer. I understand the incredible feeling of pain and injustice felt by family and friends when the killer roams free and the victim is no more among us. I can't bring my cousin back; I can't bring Andrew and Abby back from the grave either. And I certainly can't undo the gruesome events of the morning of August 4, 1892 in the Borden house. But I and you can do something, or at least keep trying to: and that is to seek a solution to this murder case. The one and only way we can bring any sense of justice and closure to this case is by caring enough to want to try and reveal the true killer's identity to posthumous shame and thus to avenge the victims whose blood cries out for the truth to be known. If through this book I have brought us even one small step closer to solving this case, I feel I have succeeded in my aim.

What I have sought to do with this book is to present all the most relevant material of both arguments for/against Lizzie as murderer and then to, well, avoid giving any biased conclusions of my own based on the theories and evidence. But I encourage you, dear reader, to study the arguments and come up with your own ideas and conclusions. Also, I have tried to present the important old evidence in a fresh new way, a simple and accessible way, a readable way suited to both novice and now-all alike, along with presenting scholarly content in the appropriate scholarly fashion, and revealing new/rare/overlooked content related to Lizzie or aspects of Bordenia. In addition, I have thrown in some fun stuff (fiction, humor and poetry) for pure entertainment. This book is a compilation of many of the facts, theories and revelations I've learned and gathered on the case in the course of my research. I was told that a portion of the Jennings Papers have never been disclosed, but I don't know if this is true. Incidentally, the Hilliard Papers are off limits to me and other researchers because they are scheduled for future publication by the Fall River Historical Society, as Michael Martins will not allow anyone to use that in manuscript form for this reason. Also, there were a few new morcels of information, a few good things I couldn't put in this book because I still haven't completed my research on it, as in the case of my two-hatchets theory; or I couldn't find anywhere to put them or didn't have enough to beef it out to a satisfactory length; for example, tidbits on Helen Pierce, Melvin Adams, Mary Colony, George Robinson, John Morse, Sarah Morse, Mary Brigham, Helen Leighton, Lucy Macomber, Norman Hall and Nellie Miller; or frankly, as in the case of suppressed "sensitive" information about John and Bridget Sullivan, David Anthony Jr., or Ernest Terry, I was either not allowed by the descendants of these people to publish it or I couldn't afford to pay the asking price for it, although I did reveal early snippets of this research on various Lizzie Borden internet message boards. But I hope to someday come to a compromise with the parties involved and to find a way to get this info out there to my fellow Bordenites. I would like to use this new unpublished information to help me write another book on Lizzie in the future or to write more articles on the case. In conclusion, I hope this has been a pleasant and thought-provoking experience for you. If so, great. If not, throw this book on the fire and have a shower to cleanse yourself of the unhappy experience.

Respectfully,

David Rehak

Did Lizzie Borden Axe For It?

Bibliography

Transcripts (source material)

A letter addressed to "Miss Emma Borden" and purporting to be written in Waltham, Massachusetts, August 17, 1892; *The Fall River Historical Society archive collection*
A letter by (Jonathan) Thayer Lincoln to Mattie Davol; *The Fall River Historical Society archive collection*
A letter dated August 22, 1897, signed "Lizzie A. Borden"; *The Fall River Historical Society archive collection*
A letter from Henry W. Clarke to Arthur Phillips dated March 28, 1938; *The Fall River Historical Society archive collection*
Inquest Upon the Deaths of Andrew J. and Abby D. Borden, August 9 - 11, 1892, Volume I & II
Knowlton/Pearson Correspondence, 1923-1930; *The Fall River Historical Society archive collection*
1871 Record of Land Transaction Deed for the Swansea Property between Andrew J. Borden and William M. Almy (grantees) and Almira Gardner, Hannah Gardner, and Irene Gray (granters); *Registry of Probate and the Registry of Deeds for Bristol County in Taunton*
Preliminary Hearing of the Lizzie Borden Murder Case, August 25 - September 1, 1892
Record of Autopsy on the body of Abby D. Borden, aged 64 years. Thursday August 11, 1892

Did Lizzie Borden Axe For It?

Record of Autopsy on the body of Andrew J. Borden, aged 69 years. Thursday August 11, 1892
Superior Court Trial Transcript of the Lizzie Borden Murder Case, June 5 - 20, 1893, Vol. 1 & 2, pp. 1-1930,
Witness Statements For the Lizzie Borden Murder Case, August 4 - October 6, 1892

Authors/Books

author unknown, *Lizzie Borden's Church - Central Congregational Church, Fall River, MA*
Brown, Arnold R., *Lizzie Borden: The Legend, The Truth, The Final Chapter*, Rutledge Hill Press, 1991
de Mille, Agnes, *Lizzie Borden: A Dance of Death*, Little & Brown Co., 1968
Engstrom, Elizabeth, *Lizzie Borden*, Tom Doherty Associates, Inc., 1991
Faderman, Lillian, *Surpassing The Love of Men: Romantic Friendship and Love Between Women From the Renaissance to the Present*, Quill, 2001
Hixson, Walter L., *Murder, Culture, and Injustice: Four Sensational Cases In American History*, University of Akron Press, 2000
Hoffman, Paul Dennis, *Yesterday In Old Fall River, A Lizzie Borden Companion*, Carolina Academic Press, 2000
Hunter, Evan, *Lizzie, A Novel*, Hui Corp Arbor House, 1984
Kent, David. *Forty Whacks: New Evidence in the Life and Legend of Lizzie Borden*, Yankee Books, 1992
Kent, David and Robert A. Flynn, *The Lizzie Borden Sourcebook*,

Did Lizzie Borden Axe For It?

Branden Publishing Co., 1992

Lincoln, Victoria, *A Private Disgrace: Lizzie Borden By Daylight*, Pyramid Books, 1969

Lunday, Todd, *The Mystery Unveiled: The Truth About The Borden Tragedy*, Providence, J. A. Reid, Printers & Publishers, 1893

Martins, Michael and Dennis Binette, editors, *The Commonwealth of Massachusetts vs. Lizzie A. Borden: The Knowlton Papers*, Fall River Historical Society, 1994

Masterton, William L., *Lizzie Didn't Do It!*, Branden Publishing, 2000

Morris, Alicia, *My Life: Loves, Happinesses and Sorrows*, Tolcott Printing Press, 1915

Pearson, Edmund L., *The Trial of Lizzie Borden*, Doubleday, Doran and Co., 1937

Phillips, Arthur Sherman, *The Phillips History of Fall River*, Dover Press, 1946

Porter, Edwin H., *The Fall River Tragedy*, J. D. Munroe Press, 1893

Radin, Edward D., *Lizzie Borden: The Untold Story*, Dell Publishing Co. Inc, 1961

Rebello, Leonard, *Lizzie Borden, Past & Present*, Al-Zach Press, 1999

Roberts, Gary Boyd, *Notable Kin*, Volume 2. New England Historic Genealogical Society, 1999

Sams, Ed, *Lizzie Borden Unlocked*, Yellow Tulip Press, 1992

Samuels, Charles and Louise Samuels, T*he Girl in the House of Hate*, Fawcett Pub. Inc., 1953

Satterthwait, Walter, *Miss Lizzie*, St. Martin's Press, 1989

Spiering, Frank, *Lizzie*, Random House, 1984

Sullivan, Robert, *Goodbye Lizzie Borden*, Stephen Green Press, 1974

Williams, Joyce G., Eric Smithburn and M. Jeanne Peterson, *Lizzie*

Did Lizzie Borden Axe For It?

Borden: A Casebook of Family and Crime in the 1890's, T. L. S. Publications, 1980

Wollstein, Hans J., *All Movie Guide*, 1999

Newspapers & Periodicals

American Heritage, July / August 1992

Associated Press, June 18, 1999

Boston Daily Globe, June 20 and 21, 1893; February 18, 1904

Boston Herald, August 5, 7, 10, and 11, 1892

Brockton Sunday Advertiser, September 13, 1992

Call-Bulletin San Francisco, October 10, 1955

Chief of Police, Vol. IV, no. 4, July / August, 1989

Fall River Daily Globe, August 6, 1892; December 10, 1896; June 2, 1927

Fall River Daily Herald, August 6 and 11, 1892

Fall River Evening News, August 10, 1892

Fall River Weekly News, October 11, 1893

Hartford Courant, May 11, 2001

Herald News, September 30, 2002

Lizzie Borden Quarterly, April 1993; January / July 2001; April / July 2003

Los Angeles Times, April 5, 1992

New Bedford Evening Standard, November 22, 1892; June 4, 1927

New York Evening News, December (?), 1909

New York Herald, August 5 and 6, 1892

New York Times, July 26, 1992

The Passing Show, Shubert Archive, Spring 1992

Did Lizzie Borden Axe For It?

Providence Evening Bulletin, May 12, 1923
Providence Journal-Bulletin, March 18, 1998
Providence Journal, June 21 and June 25, 1893; October 29, 2000
San Francisco Newsletter (undated): An American Lillie Langtry
Theatre magazine, 1920
Standard-Times, August 9, 1997
Union-News, September 27, 2001
U.S. News & World Report, August 3, 1992
Washington City Paper, August 4, 1998
Washington Post, July 13, 1998

TV & Internet

Ask Cousin Suella
Borden Mystery Forum
Famed Lizzie Borden House May Become Inn
Featured Landscape Coin Drops, Month by Month
Fall River Area Chamber of Commerce and Industry (Area Attractions)
Fall River Police Department, Lizzie's Last Will and Testament
Fall River Historical Society
Find A Grave
Historic Timeline-Chronology of Lizzie Borden
LawBuzz - Famous Trials, Lizzie Borden
Lizzie Borden
Lizzie Borden Bed and Breakfast
Lizzie Borden Myth in American Popular Culture
Our Love Is Here To Stay - Part III, 1900-1940: Life Upon The

Did Lizzie Borden Axe For It?

Wicked Stage
Profiles of Textual References, Miss Lizzie Andrew Borden
Real Mystery Behind The Fall River Murders, feminista!, Volume 4, Number 1
Shadowlands Haunted Places in Massachusetts
The American Experience: Eleanor Roosevelt (PBS documentary)
Unexplained Lizzie Borden House
Visitor's Guide to Bristol County
Who Is Lizzie Borden?
Women's History Month Collection, Episode 9, 2000
Women Writers

About the Author

DAVID REHAK is a Lizzie Borden researcher whose primary interest is in trying to uncover new, rare, or overlooked Bordenia. He is the author of several crime suspense novels, including the controversial and well-acclaimed *A Young Girl's Crimes*, and has worked with police as a freelance private detective distinguished for his strong mind and exceptional investigative skills. His articles on Lizzie Borden have appeared on various websites, including an online publication *The Hatchet*, which is exclusively dedicated to Lizzie.

When he's not writing, Rehak works as an ESL teacher at language schools (VYVA and Marlin) in the small quaint historical fort city of Uhersky Brod in the Czech Republic and is currently working on an autobiographical memoir mainly about his life and experiences in Europe.

Other books by DAVID REHAK:

A Young Girl's Crimes

Love and Madness

Poems From My Bleeding Heart

Crippled Dreams

The Forbidden: Three Novels of French Love

Printed in the United States
135368LV00006B/143/P

9 781435 711754